SIRTFOOD DIET FOR BEGINNERS

A 21 Days Meal Plan to Stimulate Skinny Genes and Lose Weight Fast while Eating Delicious Foods. Practical Diet Book for Women and Men to Activate Metabolism and Sirtuins

Lara Burns

Table of Contents

Introduction

Losing weight and developing a perfect body are some of the most common aspirations among individuals from different cultures, backgrounds, social classes, and genders around the world. Virtually everyone wants to lose weight and look trim and attractive.

All foods certified as sirtfood have all been extensively analyzed to understand their compositions and their effects on the body. One thing that has been found in all sirtfoods is that they contain a couple of compounds known collectively as polyphenols. The first sirtfood was analyzed in the 20th century, and it was the skin of red grapes used in making red wine. During the analysis of these skins, it was found out that these skins contained a polyphenol known as resveratrol. It had been noted earlier that unlike people who drink heavily alcoholic drinks, people who drink red wine do not tend to get unhealthy or overweight. Instead, red wine drinkers seemed to be svelte, fit, and naturally energetic.

Scientists dug further into how resveratrol, one of the most active compounds in red wine, could be affecting the burning of fat deposits and the maintenance of a trim body figure with a moderate muscle mass within the body. Their findings were nothing short of revolutionary. In their studies, these scientists found out that there are a set of genes located in our bodies known as sirtuins. There are seven sirtuins in total, and they all work together in a system. Each sirtuin is named in a simple manner. The first sirtuin gene is named SIRT 1, the second; SIRT 2, and the numbering goes on like that, reaching SIRT 7. SIRT 1 and SIRT 3 have been found out to be the most active genes in the family of the sirtuins.

The Sirt diet is loved by stars because it makes you lose weight without too many sacrifices, thanks to the foods that contain sirtuins. The Sirt diet is the diet that makes you lose weight without giving up the pleasures of the table. This type of low-calorie diet is based on the consumption of foods rich in sirtuins, a category of proteins with enzymatic activity that would be able to accelerate the metabolism, activating the so-called "lean gene," and was conceived by the two nutritionists Aidan Goggins and Glen Matten, authors of the book Sirt, the lean gene diet.

The Sirt diet is a food protocol that, through the intake of certain foods, promises to activate sirtuins, the so-called "thinness" genes. These "super metabolic regulators" can naturally set the metabolism in motion and, therefore, to burn fat and increase muscle mass. They also manage to modulate the sense of hunger and therefore help to eat less.

The Sirt diet, also known as Sirtfood, is the new way to lose weight without a radical diet by activating the same " lean gene " pathways usually induced by exercise and fasting. Some foods contain chemicals called polyphenols that exert slight stress on our cells, thus activating genes that mimic the effects of fasting and physical activity.

Foods rich in polyphenols, including cabbage, dark chocolate, and red wine, trigger sirtuins, special proteins that affect metabolism, aging, and mood. A diet rich in these foods starts weight loss without sacrificing muscles, maintaining optimal health. Thanks to this simple process, the Sirt diet is now in fashion, also used by celebrities and show business personalities.

Chapter 1: What Are Sirtuins

To know exactly how the sirtfood diet works, it is imperative to understand the role of sirtuins in the human body. In fact, sirtuins are known for playing an important metabolic role in most living organisms. This is why the production, utilization, and stimulation of sirtuins is now considered healthy.

In simple words, sirtuins by their composition are a type of protein present in various parts of the human cell from the nucleus to mitochondria. They are part of the genetic makeup and help in DNA repair and other cell regulation activities.

Sirtuins are also often called the "skinny genes" because of the role they can play in reducing human weight. But how these genes can make that magic happen is an important question. Biological sciences are no magic, it's all about understanding your body better and then meeting the body's needs to help boost its natural healthy activities. Similarly, when we boost the formation and stimulation of sirtuins in the cell, it automatically aids metabolism, prevents aging, and puts the body on a fast track.

Not every person is obese due to lack of exercise or the food they eat—some people have a naturally low metabolic rate and it makes it almost impossible for them to get out of the trap of obesity. By stimulating the sirtuins, we can put the body on track and make burning calories faster and use them effectively.

Sirtuins are a group of genes known as inducible genes. There are several other genes located throughout the body that work using a similar mechanism as the sirtuins. They stay, relatively hidden and unnoticed within the body. However, when a condition arises that necessitates them to swing into action, inducible genes become activated. They do not just become activated magically, however. They are activated in response to the situation that necessities their attention. You can think of them like firefighters. Firefighters do not just drive their trucks and come to your house. Your house has to be on fire, and you need to call their attention to the fire. The signal that is sent to the firemen in the form of your phone call or that of your neighbors then forces the firemen to spring into action to come and put out the fire – the incident that led to them getting invited in the first place. This analogy works very well with the sirtuins. The sirtuins remain dormant over the lives of most people because they are not activated. However, when they are activated with the right signals, sirtuins perform an extremely wonderful function – they put the entire body in survival mode and aim to save the body, just like firefighters saving a house. To help the body have as much energy as possible to survive the 'perilous' times that the sirtuins believe the body is in, these genes burn up stores of fat within the body to provide energy. The deploy mechanisms to repair and rejuvenate damaged cells, and they boost the abilities of the body's immune system, making the body even more resistant to disease.

Sirtuins manage a wide scope of procedures, including interpretation, digestion, fat assembly, neurodegeneration and maturing. The different elements of these proteins have been to a great extent attributed to their capacity to catalyze the expulsion of acetyl bunches from the lysine amino-corrosive deposits of different proteins through their deacetylase movement. However, the definite natural activity of sirtuins stays vague. For example, one sirtuin, SIRT6, which has been ensnared in genome strength, irritation, malignant growth cell digestion and even lifespan, is an extremely powerless deacetylase1. On page 110 of this issue, Jiang et al.2 report the astounding revelation that SIRT6 heartily evacuates a myristoyl gathering — a long-chain greasy acyl gathering — from lysine deposits, and that this biochemical action empowers the chemical to manage the emission of TNF-α, a cytokine protein discharged from cells during irritation.

Proteins experience and assorted cluster of compound modifications that adjust their movement. The catalysts that include and evacuate these modifications are therefore key chiefs in flagging falls. The lysine side chains of proteins can be modified by connection of a little acyl bunch called acetyl, which is one of the most widely recognized administrative modifications and is most popular for its job in controlling interpretation. Other, bigger acyl modifications of lysine buildups have been distinguished, in spite of the fact that their natural jobs are to a great extent obscure.

The greater part of the seven human sirtuins (SIRT1–7) show this run of the mill movement, albeit a few, including SIRT6, have either powerless or no deacetylase action. For example, SIRT5 specially ties to and expels succinyl and malonyl modifications from lysine3. These acyl bunches are bigger than acetyls and, in contrast to them, are adversely charged, yet they are connected to lysine by a similar sort of compound bond and are evacuated in the equivalent NAD+-subordinate enzymatic response as that catalyzed by different sirtuins.

Sirtuins are referred to go about as deacetylase proteins. (Nicotinamide is a side-effect of the response.) Jiang et al.2 report that SIRT6 specially evacuates a different, long-chain acyl gathering (myristoyl) from proteins — a finding that, together with past information, require a reclassification of sirtuins as deacylases.

The SIRT5 point of reference incited Jiang et al. to research whether the obviously powerless deacetylase action of SIRT6 likewise mirrors an inclination for other acyl-lysine substrates. Their pursuit started in vitro with the utilization of synthetically blended peptides bearing lysine modified with different acyl bunches that are known to happen in cells. The outcome was clear: SIRT6 was undeniably increasingly dynamic in evacuating the long-chain greasy acyl myristoyl and palmitoyl bunches than little acyl modifications, including acetyl gatherings.

Together with past basic studies 3,4,5 indicating how different sirtuins can suit different acyl modifications, including succinyl, malonyl and propionyl lysine, it presently appears to be certain that auxiliary highlights in the sirtuins' dynamic locales oversee the inclination of everyone for expelling a specific kind of acyl modification.

In vivo, SIRT6 is known to direct the degrees of TNF-α, which traverses the cell film and is cut by a layer related protease compound, bringing about the emission of this current cytokine's extracellular area. The cytoplasmic area of TNF-α contains two myristoylated lysine. This quickly brings up two issues: does SIRT6 expel these myristoyl modifications and, if things being what they are, is this enzymatic action by one way or another associated with TNF-α guideline?

Without a doubt, Jiang et al. discovered that the myristylation level of TNF-α in refined cells relied upon the enzymatic movement of SIRT6. Emission of TNF-α likewise required SIRT6, demonstrating that expulsion of its myristoyl bunches is a key advance in this procedure. It will be intriguing to perceive how myristylation manages emission, and whether expulsion of the myristoyl bunches causes a conformational revamp in TNF-α that permits its cleavage by the layer related protease.

Jiang and associates' discoveries set up for a few new headings wherein to explore the job of greasy acyl modifications and their guideline by sirtuins. The paper ought to be the last driving force for reclassifying sirtuins as lysine deacylases5, and not just deacetylases, to mirror the broader nature of their enzymatic movement.

Significantly, it presently appears that sirtuins differ from each other in the kind of acyl modification they specially expel from substrates, albeit current discoveries do not decide out the likelihood that a given sirtuin can evacuate a few sorts of acyl modification in vivo. This is maybe the situation for SIRT6. In spite of the fact that the compound specially expels long-chain greasy acyl modifications, its deacetylase movement has been implicated6 in modification of the DNA-related histone H3 protein. It may be the case that, in vivo, the feeble deacetylase action of SIRT6 is confined to specific substrates (as has been shown6), to exact subcellular restrictions or to specific flagging pathways. The way that SIRT6 can expel a more extensive range of acyl modifications should make it conceivable to coax out the overall commitments of these biochemical exercises to this current chemical's capacity.

It has for quite some time been a riddle why sirtuins expend the vivaciously exorbitant NAD+ cofactor, as opposed to — like different classes of deacetylase — utilizing basic hydrolysis to deacetylate substrates. Clarifications summoned incorporate the administrative ramifications of coupling sirtuin movement to the phone's metabolic state, in which NAD+ is included, or the conceivable flagging job of the O-acetyl ADP-ribose item (Fig. 1). Another clarification might be the need to create a nucleotide bearer for the leaving acyl gathering. The O-myristoyl ADP-ribose conjugation additionally forestalls myristate from getting lengthened by further enzymatic response to frame another unsaturated fat, palmitate, along these lines safeguarding the accessible pool of myristate.

O-Acetyl ADP-ribose is separated by a few enzymes7, and it is not yet clear which of them control the degrees of other O-acyl ADP-ribose items or move them to different bearers, and whether these exercises influence or even drive upstream pathways engaged with creating these metabolites. Until further notice, the disclosure of SIRT6-interceded demyristoylation opens an energizing section in the account of the seven human sirtuins and their natural action."

Sirtuins, Fasting, and Metabolic Activities

SIRT1, just like other SIRTUINS family, is protein NAD+ dependent deacetylases that are associated with cellular metabolism. All sirtuins, including SIRT1 important for sensing energy status and in protection against metabolic stress. They coordinate cellular response towards Caloric Restriction (CR) in an organism. SIRT1 diverse location and allows cells to easily sense changes in the level of energy anywhere in the mitochondria, nucleus, and cytoplasm. Associated with metabolic health through deacetylation of several target proteins such as muscles, liver, endothelium, heart, and adipose tissue.

SIRT1, SIRT6, and SIRT7 are localized in the nucleus where they take part in the deacetylation of customers to influence gene expression epigenetically. SIRT2 is located in the cytosol, while SIRT3, SIRT4, and SIRT5 are located in the mitochondria where they regulate metabolic enzyme activities as well as moderate oxidative stress.

SIRT1, as most studies with regards to metabolism, aid in mediating the physiological adaptation to diets. Several studies have shown the impact of sirtuins on Caloric Restriction. Sirtuins deacetylase non-histone proteins that define pathways involved during the metabolic adaptation when there are metabolic restrictions. Caloric Restriction, on the other hand, causes the induction of expression of SIRT1 in humans. Mutations that lead to loss of function in some sirtuins genes can lead to a reduction in the outputs of caloric restrictions. Therefore, sirtuins have the following metabolic functions: Regulation In The Liver

The Liver regulates the body glucose homeostasis. During fasting or caloric restriction, glucose level becomes low, resulting in a sudden shift in hepatic metabolism to glycogen breakdown and then to gluconeogenesis to maintain glucose supply as well as ketone body production to mediate the deficit in energy. Also, during caloric restriction or fasting, there is muscle activation and liver oxidation of fatty acids produced during lipolysis in white adipose tissue. For this switch to occur, there are several transcription factors involved to adapt to energy deprivation. SIRT1 intervenes during the metabolic switch to see the energy deficit.

At the initial stage of the fasting that is the post glycogen breakdown phase, there is the production of glucagon by the pancreatic alpha cells to active gluconeogenesis in the Liver through the cyclic amp response element-binding protein (CREB), and CREB regulated transcription coactivator 2 (CRTC2), the coactivator. Is the fasting gets prolonged, the effect is cancelled out and is being replaced by SIRT1 mediated CRTC2 deacetylase resulting in targeting of the coactivator for ubiquitin/ proteasome-mediated destruction? SIRT1, on the other hand, initiates the next stage of gluconeogenesis through acetylation and activation of peroxisome proliferator-activated receptor coactivator one alpha, which is the coactivator necessary for fork head box O1. In addition to the ability of SIRT1 to support gluconeogenesis, coactivator one alpha is required during the mitochondrial biogenesis necessary for the liver to accommodate the reduction in energy status. SIRT1 also activates fatty acid oxidation through deacetylation and activation of the nuclear receptor to increase energy production. SIRT1, when involved in acetylation and repression of glycolytic enzymes such as phosphoglycerate mutate 1, can lead to shutting down of the production of energy through glycolysis. SIRT6, on the other hand, can be served as a co-repressor for hypoxia-inducible Factor 1 Alpha to repress glycolysis. Since SIRT6 can transcriptionally be induced by SIRT1, sirtuins can coordinate the duration of time for each fasting phase.

Aside from glucose homeostasis, the liver also overtakes in lipid and cholesterol homeostasis during fasting. When there are caloric restrictions, the synthesis of fat and cholesterol in the liver is turned off, while lipolysis in the white adipose tissue commences. The SIRT1, upon fasting, causes acetylation of steroid regulatory element-binding protein (SREBP) and targets the protein to destroy the ubiquitin-professor system. The result is that fat cholesterol synthesis will repress. During the regulation of cholesterol homeostasis, SIRT1 regulates oxysterol receptor, thereby, assisting the reversal of cholesterol transport from peripheral tissue through upregulation of the oxysterol receptor target gene ATP-binding cassette transporter A1 (ABCA1).

Further modulation of the cholesterol regulatory loop can be achieved via bile acid receptor, that's necessary for the biosynthesis of cholesterol catabolic and bile acid pathways. SIRT6 also participates in the regulation of cholesterol levels by repressing the expression and post-translational cleavage of SREBP1/2, into the active form. Furthermore, in the circadian regulation of metabolism, SIRT1 participates through the regulation of cell circadian clock.

Mitochondrial SIRT3 is crucial in the oxidation of fatty acid in mitochondria. Fasting or caloric restrictions can result in upregulation of activities and levels of SIRT3 to aid fatty acid oxidation through deacetylation of long-chain specific acyl-CoA dehydrogenase. SIRT3 can also cause activation of ketogenesis and the urea cycle in the liver.

SIRT1 also Add it in the metabolic regulation in the muscle and white adipose tissue. Fasting causes an increase in the level of SIRT1, leading to deacetylation of coactivator one alpha, which in turn causes genes responsible for fat oxidation to get activated. The reduction in energy level also activates AMPK, which will activate the expression of coactivator one alpha. The combined effects of the two processes will give rise to increased mitochondrial biogenesis together with fatty acid oxidation in the muscle.

Chapter 2: Why the Sirtfood Diet Works

It is important to understand how and why it works however, so that you can appreciate the value of what you are doing. It is important to also know why these sirtuin rich foods help to help you maintain fidelity to your diet plan. Otherwise, you may throw something in your meal with less nutrition that would defeat the purpose of planning for one rich in sirtuins. Most importantly, this is not a dietary fad, and as you will see, there is much wisdom contained in how humans have used natural foods even for medicinal purposes, over thousands of years.

To understand how the Sirtfood diet works, and why these particular foods are necessary, we will look at the role they play in the human body.

Sirtuin activity was first researched in yeast, where a mutation caused an extension in the yeast's lifespan. Sirtuins were also shown to slow aging in laboratory mice, fruit flies, and nematodes. As research on Sirtuins proved to transfer to mammals, they were examined for their use in diet and slowing the aging process. The sirtuins in humans are different in the typing but they essentially work in the same ways and reasons.

There are seven "members" that make up the sirtuin family. It is believed that sirtuins play a big role in regulating certain functions of cells including proliferation reproduction and growth of cells), apoptosis death of cells). They promote survival and resist stress to increase longevity.

They are also seen to block neurodegeneration loss or function of the nerve cells in the brain). They conduct their housekeeping functions by cleaning out toxic proteins and supporting the brain's ability to change and adapt to different conditions, or to recuperate i.e., brain plasticity). As part of this they also help reduce chronic inflammation and reduce something called oxidative stress. Oxidative stress is when there are too many cell-damaging free radicals circulating in the body, and the body cannot catch up by combating them with antioxidants. These factors are related to age-related illness and weight as well, which again, brings us back to a discussion of how they actually work.

You will see labels in Sirtuins that start with "SIR," which represents "Silence Information Regulator" genes. They do exactly that, silence or regulate, as part of their functions. The seven sirtuins that humans work with are: SIRT1, SIRT2, SIRT3, SIRT4, SIRT 5, SIRT6 and SIRT7. Each of these types is responsible for different areas of protecting cells. They work by either stimulating or turning on certain gene expressions, or by reducing and turning off other gene expressions. This essentially means that they can influence genes to do more or less of something, most of which they are already programmed to do.

Through enzyme reactions, each of the SIRT types affect different areas of cells that are responsible for the metabolic processes that help to maintain life. This is also related to what organs and functions they will affect.

For example, the SIRT6 causes an expression of genes in humans that affect skeletal muscle, fat tissue, brain, and heart. SIRT 3 would cause an expression of genes that affect the kidneys, liver, brain and heart.

If we tie these concepts together, you can see that the Sirtuin proteins can change the expression of genes, and in the case of the Sirtfood diet we care about how sirtuins can turn off those genes that are responsible for speeding up aging and for weight management.

The other aspect to this conversation of sirtuins is the function and the power of calorie restriction on the human body. Calorie restriction is simply eating less calories. This coupled with exercise and reducing stress is usually a combination for weight loss. Calorie restriction has also proven across much research in animals and humans to increase one's lifespan.

We can look further at the role of sirtuins with calorie restriction and using the SIRT3 protein which has a role in metabolism and aging. Amongst all of the effects of the protein on gene expression, such as preventing cells from dying, reducing tumors from growing, etc.)

The SIRT3 has high expression in those metabolically active tissues as we stated earlier, and its ability to express itself increases with caloric restriction, fasting, and exercise. On the contrary, it will express itself less when the body has a high fat, high calorie-riddled diet.

The last few highlights of sirtuins are their role in regulating telomeres and reducing inflammation which also help with staving off disease and aging.

Telomeres are sequences of proteins at the ends of chromosomes. When cells divide these get shorter. As we age, they get shorter, and other stressors to the body also will contribute to this. Maintaining these longer telomeres is the key to slower aging. In addition, proper diet, along with exercise and other variables can lengthen telomeres. SIRT6 is one of the sirtuins that, if activated, can help with DNA damage, inflammation and oxidative stress. SIRT1 also helps with inflammatory response cycles that are related to many age-related diseases.

Calories restriction can extend life to some degree. Since this, as well as fasting, is a stressor, these factors will stimulate the SIRT3 proteins to kick in and protect the body from the stressors and excess free radicals. Again, the telomere length is affected as well.

Having laid this all out before you, you should be able to appreciate how and why these miraculous compounds work in your favor, to keep you youthful, healthy, and lean If they are working hard for you, don't you feel that you should do something too?

Why Eat Sirtfoods?

People are just starting to realize the great value of sirtuins, and they include them in their diets and meal plans. The sirtuin activators can have a huge impact on your health, and they also are effective when it comes to suppressing your appetite and building more muscle.

As previously mentioned, sirtuins represent a certain group of proteins that can be found in various foods, mostly in fruits and vegetables. Most of us can agree that you can't go wrong with eating fruits and veggies. They are a great source of minerals, vitamins, and proteins. Now, there are plenty of people who also consider the fact that these proteins are not enough to maintain your muscle mass and for your body to function properly, and I'm afraid I need to agree with them. Thus, most adults consider adding meat to their meals.

If you ask bodybuilders what they eat in order to get the required protein intake for growing their muscle mass, they will say meat, eggs, milk, and cheese. These are the food types with the highest concentration of proteins. However, proteins are very diverse and can be found in plenty of other sources, including plants, vegetables, and fruits. The sirtfood diet doesn't encourage people to consume just foods or ingredients with a high concentration of sirtuins. The founders of this diet, Aidan Goggins and Glen Matten, believe that no food should be left behind. Therefore, if sirtuins can only be found in fruits and veggies, this doesn't mean you have to become a vegetarian.

It is all about getting the right balance of ingredients and foods. You can still eat anything you want, but you need to lower the quantity of more harmful food (carbs, processed meat, and so on). As we all know, carbs can cause addiction. So why stuff ourselves with these food types? The sirtfood diet suggests replacing carbs with a special kind of protein (the sirtuin). You will notice that you will no longer become hungry (so easily), as this diet is designed to suppress your appetite. Therefore, your body will no longer crave calories from carbs, and you can easily control your calorie intake. Calorie deprivation and appetite suppression lead to weight loss, plus it leads to lower blood sugar and insulin level.

You already know that most health problems (e.g., diabetes, inflammation, and different types of cancer) are caused by poor nutrition, especially the accumulation of sugar in your blood. By consuming food rich in sirtuins, you don't have to worry about increasing your blood sugar or insulin level. Truth be told — most people are judging diets by its results in terms of weight loss. However, a diet can only be sustained for as long as it has health benefits to your body. It is pointless to stick to a radical diet if you lose a lot of weight very fast but jeopardize your health. This is why you need to seek long-term results and make the sirtfood diet your default eating habit. Basically, it has to become part of your lifestyle. We're not talking about a radical diet, as this one is pretty easy to stick to. No food is left behind, remember? You might be willing to give it a try but still not sure what to eat when following this diet. Well, you don't have to worry about this, as this book will provide you plenty of recipes and even a meal plan you can stick to.

Is It Effective?

The creators of the Sirtfood Diet make extreme cases, including that the eating routine can super-charge weight reduction, turn on your "thin quality" and forestall illnesses. The issue is there isn't a lot of verification to back them. Up until this point, there's no persuading proof that the Sirtfood Diet has a more significant impact on weight reduction than some other calorie-confined eating routine.

What's more, albeit a large number of these nourishments have fortifying properties, there have not been any long-haul human examinations to decide if eating an eating routine rich in sirtfoods has any substantial medical advantages. By the by, the Sirtfood Diet book reports the aftereffects of a pilot study led by the writers and including 39 members from their wellness place. Notwithstanding, the aftereffects of this examination show up not to have been distributed anyplace else.

For multi-week, the members followed the eating regimen and practiced day by day. Toward the week's end, members lost a normal of 7 pounds (3.2 kg) and kept up or even picked up the bulk. However, these outcomes are not astonishing. Confining your calorie admission to 1,000 calories and practicing simultaneously will almost consistently cause weight reduction. In any case, this sort of brisk weight reduction is neither certifiable nor dependable, and this examination didn't follow members after the first week to check whether they recovered any of the weight, which is regularly the situation.

At the point when your body is vitality denied, it goes through its crisis vitality stores, or glycogen, notwithstanding consuming fat and muscle. Every atom of glycogen requires 3–4 particles of water to be put away. At the point when your body goes through glycogen, it disposes of this water also. It's known as "water weight." In the first seven day stretch of outrageous calorie limitation, just around 33% of the weight reduction originates from fat, while the other 66% originates from water, muscle and glycogen. When your calorie admission expands, your body recharges its glycogen stores, and the weight returns right.

The sirtfood for Weight loss

Research conducted by Aidan Goggins and Glen Martin showed that 7 pounds of weight was lost on average in seven days on the Sirt food diet after taking note of muscle gain. Sirtuins' diet has not promised only weight loss; instead, good health as well. An increase in the level of body sirtuins has been proven to cause weight loss. The best way of increasing body leptin is still through fasting and exercise. Also, one of the best ways of enhancing body sirtuins is by consumption of sirtuin foods. All of the seas will affect the body metabolism, which we will treat in the next chapter.

Furthermore, hypothalamic SIRT1 has been proven to help in weight loss. The hypothalamus is the central weight and energy balance controller. It modulates energy intake and energy consumption by neural inputs from the periphery as well as direct humor inputs, which senses the energy status of the body. An adipokine, leptin, is one of the factors that signal that sufficient energy is stored on the periphery. Leptin plasma levels are positive for adiposity, suppressing energy intake, and stimulating energy spending. A prolonged increase in the level of plasma leptin in obese can cause leptin resistance. Leptin resistance, in turn, can affect the hypothalamus from having access to leptin, which also reduces leptin signals transduction in the hypothalamic neurons. Reduced peripheral energy-sensing by leptin can lead to a positive energy balance and incremental weight gain and adiposity improvements, which further exacerbate leptin resistance. Leptin resistance causes an increase in adiposity, just like weight gain are all associated with aging. Similar observations occur in central insulin resistance. The improvement of the action of humoral factors in the hypothalamus can, therefore, prevent progressive weight gains, especially among middle-aged individuals. SIRT1 is a protein deacetylase, NAD+ dependent, that has many substrates, such as transcription factors, histones, co-factors, and various enzymes. SIRT1 improves the sensitivity to leptin and insulin by decreasing the levels of several molecules that impair the transduction of leptin and insulin signals. The hypothalamic SIRT1 and NAD+ levels decrease with age. Increased in the level of SIRT1 has shown to improve kept in level in mice and so prevents age-related weight gain. By preventing the loss of age dependent SIRT1 hypothalamus role, there will be a boost in the activity of humoral factors in the hypothalamus and the central energy balance control.

Sirtfood for building muscle

sirtuins are a group of proteins with different effects. Sirt-1 is the protein responsible for causing the body to burn fat rather than muscle for energy, which is obviously a miracle for weight loss. Another useful aspect of Sirt-1 is its ability to improve skeletal muscle.

Skeletal muscle is all the muscles you voluntarily control, such as the muscles in your limbs, back, shoulders and so on. There are two other types, cardiac muscle is what the heart is formed of, whilst smooth muscle is your involuntary muscles – which includes muscles around your blood vessels, face and various parts of organs and other tissues.

Skeletal muscle is separated into two different groups, the blandly named type-1 and type-2. Type 1 muscle is effective at continued, sustained activity whereas type-2 muscle is effective at short, intense periods of activity. So, for example, you would predominantly use type-1 muscles for jogging, but type-2 muscles for sprinting.

Sirt-1 protects the type-1 muscles, but not the type-2 muscle, which is still broken down for energy. Therefore, holistic muscle mass drops when fasting, even though type-1 skeletal muscle mass increases.

Sirt-1 also influences how the muscles actually work. Sirt-1 is produced by the muscle cells, but the ability to produce Sirt-1 decreases as the muscle ages. As a result, muscle is harder to build as you age and doesn't grow as fast in response to exercise. A lack of sirt-1 also causes the muscles to become tired quicker and gradually decline over time.

When you start to consider these effects of Sirt-1, you can start to form a picture about why fasting helps keep the body supple. Fasting releases Sirt-1, which in turn helps skeletal muscle grow and stay in good shape. Sirt-1 is also released by consuming sirtuin activators, giving the sirtfood diet its muscle retaining power.

Who Should Try the Sirtfood Diet?

Anyone who can make the best use out of this diet should try it. There is no one formula of who should try the sirtfood diet and who shouldn't. However, based on the body's needs and the physical problems a person is suffering from, we can decide on a better utility of this diet. Following are the cases in which the sirtfood diet can prove to be most effective.

Obesity

Sirtuin burns fats quickly, and that's what makes this diet a great help for weight loss. When we study all the cases of the successful sirtfood dieters, we can clearly see how well they fought against obesity. Adele is just one example, who has amazed the world with her 30 pounds of weight loss achievement using the sirtfood diet. So, anyone who isn't able to lose some extra pounds for whatever reason, they can switch to sirtfood and then can see the magic happening.

Low or Poor Metabolic Activity

Since sirtuins are mainly responsible for better cell metabolism, lower sirtuin levels in the body can hamper the natural cell activities and hinders the metabolism. Poor metabolic activity results in weakening of physical strength, obesity, hormonal imbalance, low enzymic activity, and several other related problems. The sirtfood diet is therefore suggested to boost the metabolic rates in the body and revitalize the body and the mind with levels of energy.

No workouts

Extraneous workouts are just not for everybody. Sure, working out is a good way to lose some pounds but it is not possible for every other person to invest the required time and energy into the workouts. Therefore, the sirtfood diet can be used by such individuals. Through this diet, they can manage their weight and lose it even while doing some basic physical activities.

Aging

Aging seems like a threat to all when those wrinkles start appearing on the skin, and the person feels weakened inside out! Well, this magic gene sirtuin can also play its part in countering the effects of aging. It helps DNA to prolong its life and also aid in the repair process. Sirtuin is also responsible for apoptosis and leads to the formation of new healthy cells. This is the reason that people who are entering into middle age should consider doing the sirtfood diet so that they could effectively fight the possible signs of aging in the years to come.

Inflammation

What appears to be weight gain or metabolic inactivity is mostly connected to inflammation of both cells and organs in most cases. This inflammation is both the result and cause of several health problems. Sirtfood does not only prevent inflammation at cellular levels but effectively prevents it at the tissue and organ level.

Stress

There is one added advantage that higher sirtuin levels can guarantee and that is the reduction in stress and depression. Research is still being conducted on the relationship between sirtfood and stress, but sirtuin is that element that can enable quick brain cell recovery and boosts brain activity by getting rid of all the unwanted metabolic waste. Efficient brain functioning then leads to a reduction in stress. So, this sirtfood diet can also help with stress relief.

Burn Fat and Skinny Gene

So far, we've taken a look at the impacts of SIRT1 on fat loss on a notable kind of fat called white adipose tissue (WAT). This is the sort of fat-related to weight gain. It spends significant time away and development is appallingly obstinate and secretes a large group of fiery synthetic substances that oppose fat burning and energize further fat collection, making us overweight and stout. This is the reason weight gain regularly begins gradually, however can snowball so rapidly.

However, not exclusively does PGC-1α advance more mitochondria, it likewise urges them to burn fat as the fuel of the decision to make the energy. So, from one viewpoint, fat stockpiling is blocked, and on the other fat burning is expanded.

Ordinarily, accomplishing huge fat loss requires an impressive penance, either seriously decreasing calories or participating in superhuman degrees of activity or both.

It's just when we comprehend what befalls our fat cells when sirtuin movement is expanded that we can start to understand these astounding discoveries.

PPAR-γ (peroxisome proliferator-actuated receptor-γ). PPAR-γ coordinates the fat-gain process by turning on the genes that are expected to begin blending and putting away fat. To stop the multiplication of fat, you should cut the flexibly. Stop PPAR-γ, and you viably stop fat gain.

SIRT1 blocks the procedure of PPAR-γ. With the action of PPAR-γ stopped, SIRT1 washes down the fat in the circulation system. In addition to the fact that this is finished by closing down the creation and ability of fat, as we've seen, however, it really changes our metabolism, so we begin freeing the collection of overabundance fat. A key controller in our cells known as PGC-1α additionally helps with these procedures. This intensely animates the production of what are known as mitochondria. These are the minuscule energy manufacturing parts that exist inside every one of our cells—they power the body. The more efficient the mitochondria work, the more energy we can create.

There is also another captivating edge to the sirtuin procedure, including a lesser-known kind of fat, brown adipose tissue (BAT), which carries on in an unexpected way. In complete complexity to white fat tissue, BAT is useful to us and needs to get spent. Brown adipose tissue really encourages us to consume energy and has advanced in well-evolved creatures to permit them to scatter a lot of energy as heat. Here is the place SIRT1 initiation accomplishes something really astonishing. It turns on genes in our white fat tissue, so it transforms and assumes the properties of brown fat tissue in what is known as a "browning effect." That implies our fat stores begin to carry on in an out and out various way—rather than putting away energy, they begin to assemble it for removal.

As should be obvious, sirtuin activation has intense direct activity on fat cells, urging fat to dissolve away. However, it doesn't end there. Sirtuins additionally emphatically impact the most pertinent hormones engaged with weight control. Sirtuin activation improves insulin movement. This assists with darkinishing insulin resistance—the susceptibility of our cells to react appropriately to insulin—which is intensely involved in weight gain. SIRT1 likewise improves the discharge and movement of our thyroid hormones, which share many covering roles in boosting our metabolism and, at last, the rate at which we copy fat.

How to Hack the Skinny Genes

Genes contain data that determine everything from appearance to intelligence. An individual acquires genes from their parents, and how parents live affects their offspring's genes.

It's a mixed-up supposition that all that you acquired in your genes is changeless. Your way of life and conditions can stir singular genes or potentially smother others. Here are ways you can modify your condition and way of life to improve your body and brain.

1. Your health will depend on the type of food you eat

Food and nutrients are significant - both can impact the body and psyche. On the off chance that you consistently eat solid and nutritious food, your genes will react as needs to be. Sound sustenance stirs basic genes that positively affect your brain and body. It's basic to have a reliably sound diet since you need your great genes to be dynamic.

Keep up a truly thorough food plan consistently. Your food plan might comprise a free form of the paleo diet. In addition to the fact that this keeps will keep the brain sharp, yet it encourages and keeps up an optimal execution when working out. Try not to take alcohol, don't smoke, and don't do any form of drugs. You feel healthier than you will ever be.

2. Stress can initiate changes

Everyone manages pressure, and that can affect our health and genes. In case you're reliably worried, certain valuable genes can progressively get smothered or enacted to enable you to adapt. That can directly affect your efficiency and health.

To battle pressure, you can go on long runs or drive while tuning in to your preferred music. Utilize positive mental quality tricks and breathing activities to help still your mind and slow your pulse down.

3. A functioning way of life will stir the best genes

A functioning way of life impacts changes as well. You don't need to be an activity addict to get great outcomes. You should simply enjoy some physical movement, for example, moving or running all the time. Your body will initiate genes expected to help those exercises after some time. The effect has a net positive on your health, mind, and profitability.

4. Change your condition

Once in a while, changing your condition isn't as simple as affecting different parts of your life; however, you can control it in little manners. Normal introduction to morning daylight, a clean home environment and living close to a lush zone can impact your dynamic genes, mind, body, and even your state of mind.

Keeping the entirety of the workplace clean and mess-free, you should continually change where you work and travel. For me, the result is a substantially more gainful, unique way of life.

The Procedure of the Sirtfood Diet

One step at a time! That's what it takes to incorporate sirtfood into your diet. The diet is simple and easy to follow in a sense that it only calls for a few definite steps to take. Firstly, you will need to increase food consumption that is rich in sirtuin, then you will have to follow the phases of the diet as discussed in the next section of this book, plus you will need to add green juices to your daily diet. Here are a couple of steps that must be followed to achieve your weight loss goals on a sirtfood diet:

Get the right ingredients

Remember that all this diet asks from you is to increase your sirtuins intake. That can be done only through careful and selective grocery shopping. Prepare a list of the ingredients that contain a high amount of sirtuins and check their utility as per your meal plan. There are certain ingredients like coffee, parsley, red wine, and chocolate, that you can have all the time. So, stock up your kitchen cabinets with these ingredients.

Set up the schedule

The sirtfood diet gives you small weight loss targets for each week. In the initial time period, you must prepare a schedule to keep track of your meals, the caloric intake, and the timing of green juices you are consuming in a day. In this way, you will be able to manage the first few days of the diet adoption easily and continue observing body changes and measure your weight to keep track of your pace.

Prepare for the first week

In the first week of the sirtfood diet, the dieter must control his caloric intake. Therefore, to avoid any mistakes or confusion, all the high caloric food items should be removed from sight. Stuff your refrigerator only with the food that is appropriate for the sirtfood diet, and keep the juices, fruits, and vegetables ready to use. Instead of planning your meal every other day, make plans for the entire week according to the caloric limitations.

Caloric intake

Keep in mind that sirtfood is more about weight loss, so mere sirtuins cannot magically work overnight if you keep consuming more calories than your body can actually burn. Do the math and understand your caloric needs, even when the diet does not restrict you from high caloric intake after the first seven days. Still, you must maintain a strict check on the daily caloric intake to keep the weight in control. Otherwise, it does not take much to regain the lost pounds.

Green juices

Green juices are one of the most essential parts of the sirtfood diet. These are your way to detoxification and quick weight loss. Green veggies are full of phytonutrients, minerals, and antioxidants. Having them frequently throughout the day can help boost the metabolism, remove the metabolic waste from the body, and enables the body to metabolize the needed nutrients appropriately. These juices are also great for keeping electrolyte balance in the body.

Maintenance

To harness the benefit of this diet or any other diet for that matter, it is imperative to maintain your new dietary routine. Most people abandon the diet as soon as they are an oven with the first two phases of the diet or when they achieve their weight loss goals. And soon, they regain weight and blame the diet for being ineffective, which is far from true. It all depends on how consistently you follow this diet plan.

Chapter 3: Which Are the Sirtfoods?

1. Birds Eye Chilies

Recently, Bird's eye chilies have become very expensive and sometimes scarce in many countries around the world.

That is because people are becoming increasingly aware of the health benefits of this fruit (yes, it's a fruit not a vegetable), especially for weight loss. And unlike many other chili peppers, this one is grown in very little quantities.

Bird's eye chili has superb Sirtuin-activating properties but its benefits for weight loss don't end there.

Bird's eye chilies also play a key role in enhancing body metabolism. They contain a special compound called Capsaicin that creates a hot and burning sensation when you eat them. This raises your body's temperature and, in order to regulate the temperature, your body will resort to burning more calories to create body heat.

The result of this is a faster weight loss because your body will often have to turn to the unused, stored up fat deposits to make up for the increase in calorie consumption.

Other health benefits of the Bird's eye chili for weight loss include:

Contains Antioxidant Properties: Bird's eye chilies contain at least 4 different antioxidants, among which there are capsaicin, violaxanthin, sinaplic acid, and ferulic acid. Antioxidants also improve the body's natural metabolic processes and lead to increased weight loss.

Reduces Blood Cholesterol: Bird's eye chilies, because they contribute to the burning of old, stored up fats in the body, help to reduce the presence of the bad cholesterol, low-density lipoprotein (LDL) in the body.

Reduces Bloating and Flatulence: If you are looking to reduce the size of your tummy and waistline, you should consider adding more Bird's eye chilies to your diet. They help to stimulate the stomach and intestinal tracts, helping to promote digestion and excretion and the result is reduced bloating and a smaller waistline.

2. Buckwheat

Buckwheat is a crop that originated from Japan. In fact, legend has it that buckwheat was such a favorite amongst Buddhist Monks that sometimes, when they made long trips to the mountains, they would go with bags of buckwheat and cooking utensils so that they could cook some buckwheat whenever they get the chance.

There wasn't so much room for cooking so they often needed foods that could keep them nourished for a very long time after a single consumption and buckwheat was one of their favorites.

Buckwheat contains rutin, a chemical compound that has Sirtuin-activating properties.

But apart from being able to help you activate your skinny genes, buckwheat also has many other benefits for weight loss.

Improves Digestion: Buckwheat helps to speed up weight loss by improving metabolism and digestion.

Its high fiber content helps to increase the rate at which toxins and waste products are expelled from your digestive tracts, leading to a faster metabolism and increased weight loss.

Reduces Blood Cholesterol: With regular consumption, buckwheat can help reduce your bad cholesterol (low-density lipoprotein (LDL) levels.

Reduces Blood Sugar: It is often tagged as a 'diabetic friendly' food because it has a low glycemic rate, which means that its glucose is absorbed much more slowly, which helps keep your blood sugar levels balanced.

A balanced blood sugar level plays a significant role in weight management because reduces food cravings and your overall appetite.

Promotes Gut Flora: Buckwheat also helps to stimulate the growth of healthy bacteria in the gut, which contributes to increased food digestion and absorption, and a reduction in weight gain, especially in the stomach and waist area.

3. Medjool Dates

Medjool dates are sweet, actually extremely sweet, since they have a sugar content of about 66%. So, it's only normal that you'll be wondering what this seemingly abominable food for weight loss is doing in a weight loss diet plan.

But even though Medjool dates have a high sugar content, its high polyphenol properties make it a very great food to include in a weight loss diet because polyphenols are Sirtuin-activating.

Also, the sugar in Medjool dates is different from refined or artificial sugars, which are the ones that are often problematic.

If you have a sweet tooth, and often find it hard to do without sugars on a diet, then Medjool dates are for you. You can even have them dried and grinded, and use the powder to sweeten your teas, smoothies and cereals.

This is way healthier than using table sugar, honey, syrup, or any other sweetener with a high glycemic index.

Medjool dates also have other weight loss properties and benefits:

Prevent and Relieve Constipation: Medjool dates have a high soluble fiber content that helps bulk up your stool and make it move through your intestines faster and more easily.

If you often suffer from constipation, especially when you are on a diet, Medjool dates are good for you.

Boost Energy Levels: One common problem people face during a diet is low energy levels. Because you are not eating as much food as your body is used to, or because your foods now contain less sugars and artificial sweeteners, you may begin to experience lower energy levels or outright body weakness that makes it difficult for you to get through your daily activities.

Medjool dates contain healthy and natural glucose, fructose and sucrose that can easily be processed and utilized by your body for energy.

4. Rocket/Arugula

In some recipes you'll see it written as arugula and some recipes call it rocket – but it's the same thing. It is even called rucola, roquette, or arugula in some countries.

Whatever it is called in your country, the most important thing you need to know about this leafy green is that it is rich in Quercetin and Kaempferol, two Sirtuin-activating compounds.

The Romans and Ancient Greeks used it as a digestive aid in the past. It is also believed to have aphrodisiac properties, which led it to be banned in Monasteries during the Middle Ages.

Arugula is fantastic for helping you activate your skinny genes, but it also helps you lose weight and manage your weight in several other ways:

Has Antioxidant Properties: Arugula contains powerful antioxidant properties that promote the removal of toxins and bad cholesterol from the body.

Restores body pH levels: Arugula is an alkaline food, which means it helps reduce acidity in your body, and helps you maintain a balanced pH level.

What does that have to do with weight loss, right? A balanced pH can help you burn stored up fats faster and keep your body from accumulating fat.

It also helps to promote gut flora, and improve digestion, which contribute to weight loss.

Contains Loads of Nutrients: Arugula supplies your body with a lot of essential vitamins, nutrients and phytonutrients.

This is great for people who are into portion control or calorie counting.

It helps you get all the essential nutrients that your body needs like Vitamin K, Calcium, Magnesium, and a load of others, without eating excessively.

Fights Blood Sugar Fluctuations: Fluctuations in blood sugar levels is one of the biggest culprits of overeating, especially eating of junk or sugary foods.

Increased blood sugar levels make you crave unhealthy foods, the same way abusing drugs make you crave more drugs.

Blood sugar balancing foods like arugula helps to correct this problem by reducing sugar cravings, keeping your appetite in check, and subsequently, helping you lose weight.

5. Capers

You're probably already familiar with capers, especially if you are a pizza lover as they are often used as pizza toppings.

They are also often featured in the Mediterranean diet as they have their origin from the Mediterranean area, that is South Europe and North Africa.

Capers contain several Sirtuin-activating compounds like phenols, quercetin, kaempferol, gingketin, and isoginkgetin.

They also have other properties that contribute to weight loss such as:

Improve Fat Breakdown: Capers help improve the breakdown of fatty cells and contribute to overall weight loss.

Increase Sugar Uptake: Capers can also help slow down blood sugar fluctuations by reducing the sugar uptake in your gut.

Asides their weight loss properties, capers also have antiviral and anti-cancer properties, which make them a must-have in every diet.

6. Celery

Celery has been used to cleanse and detox the body for thousands of years. It was also used to heal liver, kidney, and gut health problems in the ancient times.

Recently, celery has become more popular amongst dieters. In fact, many people swear by the Celery Juice Diet, a detox program that has you drink celery juice every day for several days or weeks.

Celery is one of the top Sirtfoods and consuming it regularly poses a lot of health and weight loss benefits:

Dissolves Fat Cells: Celery helps to dissolve fat cells, especially those ones stored in the liver, leading to improved liver function, metabolism, and overall weight loss.

Helps with Appetite Control: When you consume celery (as veggies not as juice), it fills you up for a very long time, which leads to lesser appetite and cravings, and a reduced overall food intake.

Reduces Cholesterol Levels: Celery can also lead to a significant reduction in overall cholesterol levels.

7. Cocoa

Who doesn't love a diet that allows you to have chocolate? Other diets may require that you stay far away from it, but on the Sirtfood diet you get to have as much as you want because cocoa, the major ingredient in chocolate, has Sirtuin-activating properties.

But you can't have just any chocolate you may find on the supermarket shelf.

You can only have brands that contain 85% cocoa solids or more.

Brands with fewer cocoa solids have diminished Sirtuin-activating properties and cannot be classified as Sirtfoods.

Other benefits of cocoa for weight loss include:

Promotes Sleep and Reduces Stress Levels: Stress contributes to overeating and lack of sleep contributes to weight gain.

Cocoa helps to calm the nerves and reduces stress levels and anxiety, leading to enhanced sleep and healthier eating habits.

Promotes Digestion and Excretion: Cocoa is also rich in fiber and flavonoids that contribute to detoxification and elimination of toxins and waste from the body.

Improves Metabolism: Cocoa is also a thermogenic enhancer. It helps to improve weight loss by increasing the rate at which your body utilizes calories for energy.

8. Coffee

You probably wouldn't have guessed that coffee could make it on the list of foods with 'health benefits' especially since they are often demonized because of their caffeine content.

"Caffeine is bad for you", they say; "Choose decaffeinated beverages", they advise.

While it is true that caffeine is not good for everyone, it is not true that caffeine is dangerous or shouldn't be consumed at all.

Coffee is not just one of the most powerful Sirtfoods, it also contains chlorogenic acid, a chemical compound that helps to slow down the production of glucose in the body.

Other benefits of coffee for weight loss include:

Reduces the Production of New Fat Cells: Coffee reduces the rate at which new fat cells are produced in your body, leading to reduced fat storage and increased fat loss.

Has Antioxidant Properties: If you are a frequent coffee drinker, you probably already know this. Coffee speeds up digestion and excretion and increases the rate at which toxins are expelled from your body.

Suppresses Hunger: Coffee also helps to suppress hunger. It contains chemical compounds that when absorbed in the blood stream, helps to create feelings of fullness in the gut.

Decreases Water Weight: Coffee acts as a diuretic, which means it makes you urinate often, leading to a reduction of excess fluid retention, and water weight in your body.

Of course, like I mentioned earlier, coffee is not for everyone especially if you have underlying health issues that make coffee a health risk for you.

If you can't have caffeine, it's okay to leave coffee out of your diet − you'll still have more than a dozen other Sirtfoods to choose from.

But if you are allowed to have decaffeinated coffee, you can opt for that because decaf coffee contains peptide tyrosine, a chemical compound that reduces hunger, and increases satiety.

9. Extra Virgin Olive Oil

On the Sirtfood diet, you will have to ditch all other cooking oils and start making your food exclusively with Extra Virgin Olive Oil.

Extra Virgin Olive Oil contains Sirtuin-enhancing properties, and has other benefits for weight loss including:

Contains Oleic Acid: Olive oil has oleic acid, which helps it to retain all of its antioxidant properties.

Enriched with Monounsaturated Fatty Acids: Unlike many other cooking oils that contain saturated fats which make them unhealthy for cooking and frying, Extra Virgin Olive oil is a healthier choice as it contains Monounsaturated Fatty Acids, which experts have labeled 'the good fat'.

10. Matcha Green Tea

Another super Sirtfood is Matcha green tea. Green tea, especially Matcha green tea, contains catechins, a group of powerful flavonoids that promote fat loss.

One type of catechins that is primarily found in Matcha green tea, Epigallocatechin Gallate (EGCG), is indeed a Sirtuin activator.

Matcha is processed in a particular way which makes it retain its EGCG properties, unlike other types of green tea.

Green tea also promotes weight loss and weight management due to the fact that:

Improves Breakdown of Fat Cells: Before your body can burn down the excess fat that it has accumulated over time, it must first break down the fat cells.

Some special foods such as green tea however contribute to the breakdown of fat cells by inhibiting norepinephrine, an enzyme that often prevents easy breakdown of fat cells.

Improves Fat Burning During Workout: If you have an active lifestyle or you work out regularly, consuming Matcha green tea will help to increase the rate at which your body burns fat during physical activities.

Reduces Appetite: Just like coffee, Matcha green tea suppresses your appetite and helps you make healthier food choices.

Helps Burn Stubborn Abdominal Fat: We all know how tough it can be to lose belly fat, the type of fat that lodges in your stomach, but Matcha green tea has been proven to be helpful for getting rid of this type of fat.

11. Kale

Everyone loves and eats kale, or don't we all? Well, we all should because kale is another super Sirtfood, thanks to its quercetin and kaempferol contents.

Kale is also great for weight loss because it:

 Acts as a Hunger Suppression: A single cup of kale has around 2.4 g of dietary fiber, and as you already know by now, fiber keeps you filled up for a very long time and prevents hunger.

 Contains Glucosinolate and Sulphur Compounds: Kale is filled with two very strong detoxifiers – sulphur compounds and glucosinolate.

 Both help to rid the body of toxins that make it harder for your body to break down and utilize stored up fats.

 Has Low Energy Density: Researchers have revealed that consuming foods with low energy density like kale can help you lose weight faster.

In one study conducted on a group of 200 obese women, the researchers found that subjects who consumed 2 servings of low energy-dense soup everyday lost 50% more weight compared to people who consumed high energy-dense foods.

In simpler words, it means that if I consume 3 meals of 250 calories each (750 calories in total), but with fewer kilocalories per gram, and you consume the same quantity of meals with similar calorie count but with a higher count of kilocalories per gram, I will most likely lose weight faster than you even though we're pretty much eating the same number of calories daily.

12. Lovage /Sea Parsley

It is important to not confuse lovage with flat-leaf parsley.

If you live in the US, you're probably more familiar with flat-leaf parsley, which is commonly used to garnish and spice up your meals.

But lovage is another member of the parsley family that is also known as sea parsley. Take note of this when you go grocery shopping so you can buy the right 16

Type of parsley.

Lovage contains apigen, another superb Sirtuin-activator. Lovage is also great for people who suffer from insomnia as apigen can bind to the benzodiazepine receptors in the human brain, helping to calm you down and promote sleep.

In addition to be a Sirtfood, lovage also helps with:

Digestion: Lovage promotes digestion and gastrointestinal health. It also reduces stomach bloating and gastrointestinal inflammation.

Kidney Health: A healthy functioning kidney is crucial to weight loss and weight management and lovage helps to promote kidney health by promoting detoxification and urination.

And you know what the best thing about lovage's diuretic effect is? It doesn't cause electrolytes loss like most diuretics do.

13. Red Chicory

Red chicory is a common secret ingredient in many weight loss herbal teas and supplements.

It is a Sirtuin-activator, and it also has many other weight loss benefits.

Contains Inulin: Red chicory is made up of 68% inulin, a type of carbohydrate that acts as a prebiotic.

It feeds the good bacteria in your gut, which is very important because these good bacteria help to fight off the bad bacteria that are often responsible for inflammation and many other digestive issues.

Improves Blood Sugar Control: Inulin also helps to improve blood sugar balance. It promotes carbohydrate absorption and helps to prevent blood sugar fluctuations.

Regulates Appetite: A group of researchers conducted a study where they placed 48 obese adults on 21 g of red chicory-derived oligofructose daily for 12 weeks.

They discovered that that oligofructose helped to reduce ghrelin, the hormone that stimulates hunger.

The participants reported less hunger and cravings and had better control of their appetite.

14. Red Endive

Red endives are rich in luteolin, another Sirtuin-activating compound. It helps to activate your skinny gene, and also helps with:

Helps to Keep Energy Levels Stable: Any successful weight loss program must have this important element. It must be able to keep your energy levels balanced.

If your energy levels keep fluctuating, it is unlikely that you'll be able to follow through with the diet and red chicory really helps with balancing your energy levels.

Slows Down Digestion: Red chicory also helps to slow down digestion, not in the way that you get constipated, but in a way that keeps you satiated for longer periods and keeps your appetite in check.

Rich in Antioxidants: Endives are also rich in powerful chemical compounds that neutralize free radicals and prevent cell damage.

15. Red Onions

The aromatic effect of red onions in your meals is enough reason for anyone to fall in love with them but its benefits surpass food flavoring.

Red onions are a rich source of the Sirtuin-activating compound, quercetin. In fact, of all the foods on this list, red onions have the highest amount of quercetin in them.

Other reasons why red onions are great for weight loss include:

Powerful Probiotic Food: Red onions, just like red chicory, contribute to gut health as they help to feed the good bacteria in your gut. This helps to prevent bloating and reduce abdominal fat.

Good Source of Fiber: Red onions are also a great source of fiber and help to reduce hunger and regulate appetite.

16. Red Wine

A diet that allows you to drink alcohol, who would have thought?

The Sirtfood diet is not one of those diets that won't allow you to have alcohol.

On this diet you can drink a glass of red wine daily as red wine is also Sirtuin-activating.

Women can have one 5-ounce glass of red wine, while men can have up to two 5-ounce glasses of red wine every day. You can also cook with it too.

Recommended red wine brands for the Sirtfood diet include Merlot, Pinot noir, and Cabernet Sauvignon.

17. Soy

Soy is a rich source of the Sirtuin activator, daidzein. It is also rich in another Sirtuin activator, formononetin.

However, you must avoid heavily processed soy products and opt for natural sources like tofu, miso, tempeh, and natto as the natural, unprocessed ones retain the Sirtuin-activating compounds you need.

Soy also promotes:

Satiety: Soy is rich in proteins, and it is a well-known fact that protein is very great for suppressing your appetite.

Appetite Control: Soy has a low glycemic index and can help with hunger prevention and appetite control.

18. Strawberries

Strawberries are great Sirtuin-activators too as they contain the plant compound, fisetin.

Strawberries also promote weight loss by:

Boosting Metabolism: Strawberries are rich in anthocyanins, another chemical compound that promotes the production of adiponectin, a hormone that helps to speed up metabolism and weight loss.

Helping to Reduce Fat: Strawberries are also rich in gallic acid which promotes the normal functioning of weight reducing hormones that are often blocked by chronic inflammation.

19. Turmeric

Turmeric contains curcumin. Curcumin is another Sirtuin-activating compound.

However, for your body to be able to properly and effectively absorb curcumin from turmeric, you have to combine it with black pepper, or cook it in fat or add it to a liquid or teas. This helps to promote the absorption of curcumin in your body.

Turmeric also aids:

Prevention of Metabolic Syndrome: Metabolic syndrome is often characterized by fat accumulation around your abdomen and is caused by insulin resistance.

Turmeric helps to prevent and control metabolic syndrome by controlling blood sugar levels, cholesterol, and triglycerides.

Increases Bile Production: Turmeric increases production of bile in the stomach, which helps to aid food digestion.

20. Walnuts

Walnuts are often listed as one of the top nuts for weight loss and rightly so. Walnuts are Sirtuin-activating, help suppress hunger, and help with appetite control.

Other sirtfoods

There are a lot of other foods out there that produce moderate levels of sirtuin-activating nutrients. The sirtfood is all about inclusion so you are free to incorporate a variety of foods with sirtuin-activators in moderation. The more sirtfoods included in your diet the better. This enables you to include more of your favorite foods to derive the maximum satisfaction and pleasure from your meal.

To maintain and continue your weight loss and wellbeing, you are encouraged to include these foods as you expand the skills of your diet

Vegetables: artichokes, asparagus, bok choy/pakchoi, broccoli, frisée, green beans, shallots, watercress, white onions, yellow endive.

Nuts and seeds: chestnuts, chia seeds, peanuts, pecan nuts, pistachio nuts, sunflower seeds

Grains and pseudo-grain: popcorn, quinoa, whole-wheat flour

Beans: fava beans, white beans (e.g., cannellini or navy)

Beverages: black tea, white tea

Chapter 4: The Benefits of the Sirtfood Diet

Yes, you would lose weight, and you would be able to fit in your skinny jeans, and your friends wouldn't be able to hide their shock and admiration when they see the new you, and maybe you would even make headlines like our dear singer Adele, but that is not where the benefits of this diet ends. Along with weight loss and weight management, the Sirtfood diet also offers a lot of health benefits.

The Health Benefits of the Sirtfood Diet

These are all the benefits you will enjoy following the Sirtfood diet:

- Muscle Gain: This is everyone's dream - we all want to lose weight without losing muscle tone. We don't want the loose skin and flabby abs, stomachs, and breasts that drastic weight loss often leaves behind.
- The Sirtfood diet will help you achieve this dream because it incorporates a lot of proteins in your daily diet, which help to promote muscle gain during fat loss.
- Diabetes: If you are suffering from diabetes or already showing symptoms of pre-diabetes, this diet can help to reboot your body and stop insulin resistance, which is often a precursor to diabetes.
- Memory Improvement: Some of the meals you'll be having on this diet, such as turmeric, are known to help with cognition problems and help with memory improvement.
- Lowers Blood Pressure and Improves Cardiovascular Health: By helping to rid the body of bad cholesterol and triglycerides that often block the arteries and make it harder for your body to pump blood, leading to high blood pressure.
- Boosts Energy: The Sirtfood diet, unlike many other diets that leave you feeling weak and under-motivated, helps to boost your energy levels 29
- Along with improving concentration so that it is easier for you to be productive and be your usual self even though you are on a diet.
- Appetite Control: Inability to control appetite is often a clog in the wheel of progress on any weight loss diet.
- Sirtuins will not only help you control your appetite by reducing blood sugar spikes, but it will also help to improve hormone balance so that your hunger and satiety hormones, ghrelin and leptin can start working normally again.
- Healthy Hair, Skin and Nails: Most of the Sirtfoods contain ingredients that help to boost hair, nail and skin health so get ready to glow and have better hair and nails on this diet.
- Boosts Fertility: This diet is also rich in vegetables, fruits and superfoods that are known to help boost fertility.
- It can also help to reverse the symptoms of Polycystic Ovary Syndrome (PCOS), which is often linked to obesity and excess weight.

Chapter 5: A 21 Days Sirt-food Diet Meal Plan

Experts in psychology have proven repeatedly over the years that it takes 21 days for the average human being to build a habit, and 90 days for that habit to become fully incorporated into his lifestyle. Building a habit can be challenging if you do not have a solid game plan, and that is our ambition for this chapter. In this chapter, we would build a 21-days sirtfood timetable that would help you get through Phases One and Two of the Sirtfood diet. Let's get moving!

DAYS	BREAKFAST	LUNCH	DINNER	SNACKS/DESSERTS
1	Chocolate Granola	Butternut pumpkin with buckwheat	Tofu Thai Curry	Chocolate Maple Walnuts
2	Oatmeal Pancakes	Roasted Artichoke Hearts	Beef bourguignon with Mashed potatoes and kale	Matcha and Chocolate Dipped Strawberries
3	Cinnamon Quinoa	Beef Broth	Turkish fajitas	Vegan Rice Pudding
4	Buckwheat Porridge	Salmon and Capers	Sirt Chicken Korma	Plum Oat Bars
5	Chocolate Granola	Pasta Salad	Tomato Chicken Mix	Spinach and Kale Mix
6	Apple Pancakes	Sirtfood Caramel Coated Catfish	Chicken and Veggies	Kale Dip with Cajun Pita Chips
7	Breakfast Muesli	Lentil Tacos	Japanese Chicken Thighs	Triple Chocolate Chip Deep Dish Cookies
8	Sirtfood Scrambled Eggs	Lentil and Quinoa Salad	Air Fried Whole Chicken	Protein Brownies

9	Strawberry Buckwheat Pancakes	Sloppy Joes	Perfect Garlic Butter Steak	Protein Pumpkin Spiced Donuts
10	Blackcurrants Pancakes	Lentil Burgers	Crispy Pork Medallions	Wrapped Plums
11	Creamy Coconut Porridge	Potato Salad	Prawns, Pak Choi and broccoli	Cucumber Sandwich Bites
12	Salmon & Kale Omelet	Ginger Brown Rice	Cocoa spaghetti Bolognese	Cocoa and Nuts Bombs
13	Sirtfood Green Onion and Mushroom Omelet	Pasta with kale and Black Olive	Baked salmon with Watercress sauce and Potatoes	Sweet Cinnamon Peaches
14	Buckwheat Granola	Asparagus Soup	Coq au vin with potatoes and green beans	Chocolate strawberry milk
15	Sirtfood Muffins	Kale White Bean Pork chops	Beans & Kale Soup	Green tea and Rocket smoothie
16	Fruity Tofu Smoothie	Tuna Salad	Beef bourguignon with Mashed potatoes and kale	Chocolate strawberry milk
17	Black currants and oat yogurt	Turkey Curry	Barbecued Lime Shrimp	Pineapple Lassi
18	Easy Granola Clusters	Tofu and Curry	Crispy Shrimp	Sirt shot
19	Stovetop Granola	Chicken and Bean Casserole	Spicy Air-Fried Cheese Tilapia	Hot chocolate eggnog
20	No Bake Peanut Butter Granola Bars	Prawn and Coconut Curry	Cheese Salmon	Mint julep
21	Banana Muesli with Dates	Moroccan Chicken Casserole	Herb Salmon Fillet	Gingerbread latte

27

Chapter 6: Phase 1 of the Sirtfood Diet: Restriction

The first stage of the sirtfood is known as the first phase, or more commonly, 'Phase 1'. Phase 1 is basically the first seven days of the sirtfood diet regimen. Phase 1 is the most intense phase of the sirtfood diet as it is the only phase where you cannot consume above a specified number of calories. In the first three days of phase 1, the maximum permissible number of calories that can be consumed per day is one thousand. In the last four days, the maximum permissible number of consumable calories moves up to 1500. The ambition of the first phase of the sirtfood diet is to help you hit the ground running and activate your sirtuin genes. The restricted number of calories will aid in the activation of your body's stress pathways, which would eventually, together with the action other polyphenols in the sirtfoods, lead to the activation of the sirtuin genes.

At the conclusive end of the first phase, the average mass of fat that would be lost should be between 5 to 7 pounds. However, your body is most likely going to retain all of its muscle or even add up some more, so using a weighing scale to judge the progress of phase 2 might not be such a good idea. So, phase 1 is basically the first seven days of your sirtfood diet.

How do you prepare for phase 1?

When you start out on the sirtfood diet, you are preparing to begin a journey to a new kind of freedom and liberation – freedom from your self-imposed shackles of poor eating habits into a world where you have control over what goes in your body. To get started out for phase 1, you will need to put a couple of things in place. These include:

A juicer: A lot of modern households already use a juicer in one way or the other on a fairly regular basis. The juicer would be used in the preparation of the sirtfood green juice, a natural concoction of herbs that would help detoxify your body and get you started on dissolving those fatty deposits. Since the aim of the juicer is to extract as much liquid as possible from vegetables, be sure to get one that is better equipped for the type of food products you would be putting in it.

Secondly, you would need to get familiar with your sirtfood menu and see where exactly you can get all these foods in your neighborhood. Depending on your city, you may be able to get all the sirtfoods you need in your local grocery store, or you may need to try shopping in the open market to get some of the vegetables and food items on the list. The point, however, is to get familiar with the foods that will be forming your new regimen and to figure out how you'd be sourcing these foods.

Thirdly, you need to figure out a means of preserving the foods you'd be purchasing beforehand. If you have steady access to electricity and a refrigerator, it is advised that you shop for three days' worth of vegetable supplies at once and store the veggies in your fridge for when you need to make your meals. After three days, you'd need another supply of veggies. The three-day limit is set to prevent spoilage of the veggies, which would only affect the quality of your food and the rate of your development.

It is also pertinent for you to learn how to prepare the foods you would prepare beforehand. The sirtfood menu features a variety of food options, so it's okay for you to select a few that you can confidently cook right away. As you progress in your journey in the diet, you will gradually learn how to cook more foods and expand your diet.

Next, it is also critically important for you to plan your eating timetable beforehand. Your sirtfood green juice should be consumed three times per day in the first three days – once when you wake up, thirty minutes to one hour before any meal, and then two other times within the day. Look at your number of calories and plan out when you would be eating and what you would be eating on each day. This will make it an effortless route for you to make these decisions when you finally begin your diet.

Journaling can be very helpful in helping you stay steadfast on your personal journey. Keeping a journal allows you to keep a chronological record of your struggles and your victories as you go through the sirtfood diet. Trying to use the scales to monitor your progress, especially so early into your dieting journey, is a bad idea. As has been repeatedly mentioned, the sirtfood diet helps you to burn fats as well as maintain and even build muscle mass. So, as you gear up to begin phase 1 of your diet, try as much as possible to stay off the scales for the meantime and just focus on sticking to this wonderful dieting system.

Finally, get excited about the journey ahead. To accomplish this, it helps if you can figure out exactly why you are embarking on the sirtfood diet. Are you doing it to reduce your risk of contracting a dangerous life-threatening disease along the line? Are you doing it to enhance your career in the media or modeling industry? Are you doing it to improve your mental health and improve your moods, focus, and concentration? Whatever be your reason for wanting to make the important personal sacrifice of starting up the sirtfood diet, remind yourself that you are finally about to achieve those aims. Be excited that your life is about to experience a positive turn around.

Expectations for Phase 1

You may wonder – what exactly is Phase 1 going to entail, and what results can I expect to achieve after the first week of my diet? With great sacrifice, they say, comes great rewards. Phase 1 is going to be the most tasking phase of your diet, no doubt, but it will also be the phase that provides you with the most pleasantly surprising results. At the end of phase 1, you can expect to lose between 5 to 7 pounds of weight in pure fat, as evidenced by the results of the cohort study carried out in London. You can also expect to experience enhanced mental clarity and focus, and a general feeling of lightness and agility. However, since phase 1 is going to be your stage of making the most important sacrifices for future benefits, it also means you would probably have to deal with some discomfort during this phase. Not everybody would experience these signs, but some participants in the diet have reported feelings of hunger, lethargy, slight irritability, and even strong cravings for junk food and sugary snacks and drinks during the first phase. It is believed that the restriction of the calories consumed by the participant in the first three days to one thousand calories, and to fifteen hundred calories in the last four days of phase one is responsible for these challenges.

So, if you feel really hungry, tired, or extremely desirous of junk food during your first phase, be patient. Remember your reason for starting this and renew your resolve to stay strong and fight for the dazzling life you've dreamed of every single day. Usually, in the final days of phase one, as your body gets used to the diet, you will feel your fatigue and tiredness slipping away, and these feelings would become replaced by feelings of strength, clarity, and agility. As you switch from one thousand calories to fifteen hundred calories per day, you will feel more satiated and energized too, and your moods will generally improve. From this point onwards, your journey becomes progressively easier.

Meal plan for Phase 1

For the first three days of the sirtfood diet, you will be expected to drink three sirtfood juices and eat one mail sirtfood meal per day. This combination helps to keep the number of calories consumed just under one thousand. For the last four days of the first phase, however, you will be required to eat two main sirtfood meals and two sirtfood juices on a daily basis. This combination would sum up to about fifteen hundred calories.

As you can probably already predict, the sirtfood green juice would be an essential part of your sirtfood diet in phase one and beyond. After water, this drink would constitute a major percentage of your total fluid intake as you proceed with the sirtfood diet. Other fluids that you would be permitted to consume would include black coffee (i.e., without milk) and green tea. Milk should be abstained from during the first phase of the sirtfood diet as it contains active substances that may hamper the activation of the sirtuin genes.

Since the sirtfood green juice is so critical to the success of your sirtfood diet, let's examine exactly how to make the sirtfood green juice before delving into what your model meal plan should look like.

To prepare the sirtfood green juice, you'll need:

2.5 oz. kale

1 oz. arugula

0.25 oz. flat-leaf parsley

5.5 oz. celery stalks (with leaves)

0.5 medium green apple

1 in. ginger

Half of a lemon squeezed or juiced.

0.5 tsp. matcha powder

Note that the matcha powder should only be included only in the first two juices of the day during the first three days of phase one. Basically, between day 1 and 3, only the juice you'd be drinking very early in the morning before breakfast, and the drink you'll be having by midmorning should contain matcha. Your third sirtfood juice of the day should not contain matcha powder because the substance has been found to be caffeinated and may alter your sleep pattern if taken too late in the day. So, do not forget – no matcha for the last juice of the day between days 1 and 3.

For the final four days of phase one, however, it is okay to put matcha powder in the two sirtfood juices you'll be drinking daily. This is because you'd have completed your daily required sirtfood juice intake by midday, provided you follow the laid-down guidelines.

So, now that you know the ingredients and you know the sirtfood juice rules let's get into the nitty-gritty of making this wonderfully wholesome drink.

First of all, mix your veggies in the juicer. This means your arugula, kale, and parsley should be loaded into the juicer. Ensure to extract as much fluid as possible from these greens to ensure that you get maximum value for your time, effort, and money. After the juicing process, you should have obtained about a quarter of a cup of veggie juice. Absolutely delicious, yeah?

The next step is to lead your apples, ginger, and celery into the juicer and extract the fluid from those too. Add this new mixture to the one obtained in the first step.

Next, peel your lemon, cut it in half, and squeeze out the juice. If you feel that your squeezing is not efficient enough, you can use the juicer instead. After adding the lemon juice to your mixture, you should have about a cup of juice ready.

Pour out a small portion of your juice and add in your half teaspoon of matcha powder. Ensure that the matcha dissolves properly in the juice, and then pour the matcha-containing juice into the rest of the juice.

Stir your juice properly, and you may add a little water to adjust the taste if you like. Enjoy the immaculate taste of good health!

Now that you have gotten a good grasp of how to make your sirtfood green juice, it's time to design a workable meal plan that would allow you to access a variety of sirtfoods to aid your progress in phase 1. Remember that in each day for your first three days, you must drink a cup of sirtfood green juice thrice and eat a sirtfood main meal once. For the remaining four days of Phase 1, its two sirtfood juices and two main meals to give fifteen hundred calories.

Let's break the meal plan down now.

Day 1: Sirtfood green juice – 3 times Main meal – 1 time

Meal idea: Stir-fried Asian shrimp, buckwheat noodles and dark chocolate (85% cocoa) Vegan option: Sesame glazed tofu, miso, ginger, chili, stir-fried greens, and dark chocolate (85% cocoa).

Day 2: Sirtfood green juice – 3 times Main meal: 1 time

Meal idea: Aromatic chicken breast, kale, red onions, tomato, and chili salsa Vegan option: Kale, red onion dal, and buckwheat.

Day 3: Sirtfood green juice – 3 times Main meal: 1 time

Meal idea: Turkey escalope, capers, sage, parsley, cauliflower, and dark chocolate.

Vegan option: Baked tofu, cauliflower, and dark chocolate.

From day four onwards, you can eat ½ oz. Dark chocolate once a day, preferably alongside one meal.

Day 4: Sirtfood green juice – 2 times Main meal: 2 times

Meal 1: Sirt muesli

Meal 2: Salmon fillet, endive, arugula, and celery salad.

Vegan option 1: Sirt muesli

Vegan option 2: Tuscan bean stew.

Day 5: Sirtfood green juice – 2 times Main meal: 2 times

Meal 1 (Vegan and regular diets): Sirt super salad.

Meal 2 (regular diet): Grilled beef, red wine, onion rings, garlic, kale, and roasted potatoes.

Meal 2 (Vegan diet): Kidney bean mole and baked potatoes.

Day 6: Sirtfood green juice – 2 times Main meal: 2 times

Meal 1: Sirtfood omelet

Meal 2: Baked chicken breast, parsley pesto, red onion salad.

Vegan option 1: Waldorf salad.

Vegan option 2: Roasted eggplants, walnuts, parsley pesto, and tomato salad.

Day 7: Sirtfood green juice – 2 times Main meal: 2 times

Meal 1: Strawberry buckwheat salad

Meal 2: Baked cod marinated in miso, sesame, and stir-fried greens Vegan option 1: Strawberry buckwheat salad.

Vegan option 2: Buckwheat noodles in miso broth, tofu, celery, and kale.

Breakfasts

Chocolate Granola

Preparation Time: 10 minutes

Cooking Time: 38 minutes

Servings: 8

Ingredients:

- ¼ cup cacao powder
- ¼ cup maple syrup
- 2 tablespoons coconut oil, melted
- ½ teaspoon vanilla extract
- 1/8 teaspoon salt
- 2 cups gluten-free rolled oats
- ¼ cup unsweetened coconut flakes
- 2 tablespoons chia seeds
- 2 tablespoons unsweetened dark chocolate, chopped finely

Directions:

1. Preheat your oven to 300°F.
2. Line a medium baking sheet with parchment paper.
3. In a medium pan, add the cacao powder, maple syrup, coconut oil, vanilla extract and salt and mix well.
4. Now, place pan over medium heat and cook for about 2-3 minutes or until thick and syrupy, stirring continuously.
5. Remove the pan of mixture from the heat and set aside.
6. In a large bowl, add the oats, coconut and chia seeds and mix well.
7. Add the syrup mixture and mix until well combined.
8. Transfer the granola mixture onto a prepared baking sheet and spread in an even layer.
9. Bake for approximately 35 minutes.
10. Remove the baking sheet from oven and set aside for about 1 hour.
11. Add the chocolate pieces and stir to combine.
12. Serve immediately.

Nutrition:

Calories 193

Total Fat 9.1 g

Saturated Fat 5.2 g

Cholesterol 0 mg

Sodium 37 mg

Total Carbs 26.1 g

Fiber 4.6 g

Sugar 5.9 g

Protein 5 g

Oatmeal Pancakes

Preparation Time: 15 minutes

Cooking Time: 5 minutes

Servings: 8

Ingredients:

- 1 cup whole wheat pancake mix
- 1/8 cup chopped walnuts
- ¼ cup old-fashioned oats

Directions:

1. Make the pancake mix according to the directions on the package.
2. Add walnuts, and oats.
3. Coat a skillet with cooking spray.
4. Add about ¼ cup of the batter onto the griddle when hot.
5. Turn pancake over when bubbles form on top.
6. Cook until golden brown.
7. Serve immediately.

Nutrition:

Calories - 155

Fat - 4 g

Carbs – 28 g

Protein – 7 g

Cinnamon Quinoa

Preparation Time: 5 minutes

Cooking Time: 6 minutes

Servings: 4

Ingredients:

- Chopped walnuts
- 1 ½ cup water
- Maple syrup
- 2 cinnamon sticks
- 1 cup quinoa, washed and drained

Directions:

1. Prepare your pressure cooker with a trivet and steaming basket.
2. Place the quinoa, and the cinnamon sticks in the basket and pour the water, then close and lock the lid.
3. Cook at high pressure for 6 minutes. When the cooking time is up, release the pressure using the quick-release method.
4. Fluff the quinoa with a fork and remove the cinnamon sticks.
5. Divide the cooked quinoa among serving bowls and top with maple syrup and chopped walnuts.

Nutrition:

Calories - 160

Fat - 3 g

Carbs – 28 g

Protein – 6 g

Buckwheat Porridge

Preparation Time: 10 minutes

Cooking Time: 15 minutes

Servings: 2

Ingredients:

- 1 cup buckwheat, rinsed
- 1 cup unsweetened almond milk
- 1 cup water
- ½ tsp. Ground cinnamon
- ½ tsp. vanilla extract
- 2 tbsp. raw honey
- ¼ cup fresh blueberries

Directions:

1. In a pan, add all the ingredients (except honey and blueberries) over medium-high heat and bring to a boil.
2. Reduce the heat to low and simmer, covered for about 10 minutes.
3. Stir in the honey and remove from the heat. Set aside, covered, for about 5 minutes.
4. With a fork, fluff the mixture, and transfer into serving bowls.
5. Top with blueberries and serve.

Nutrition:

Calories - 358

Fat - 4.7 g

Carbs – 3.7 g

Protein – 12 g

Chocolate Granola

Preparation Time: 10 minutes

Cooking Time: 38 minutes

Servings: 8

Ingredients:

- ¼ cup cacao powder
- ¼ cup maple syrup
- 2 tbsp. Coconut oil, melted
- ½ tsp. vanilla extract
- 1/8 tsp. salt
- 2 cups gluten-free rolled oats
- ¼ cup unsweetened coconut flakes
- 2 tbsp. chia seeds
- 2 tbsp. unsweetened dark chocolate, chopped finely

Directions:

1. Preheat your oven to 300ºF and line a medium baking sheet with parchment paper.
2. In a medium pan, add the cacao powder, maple syrup, coconut oil, vanilla extract, and salt, and mix well.
3. Place a pan over medium heat and cook for about 2–3 minutes, or until thick and syrupy, stirring continuously.
4. Remove from the heat and set aside. In a large bowl, add the oats, coconut, and chia seeds and mix well.
5. Add the syrup mixture and mix until well combined.
6. Transfer the granola mixture onto a prepared baking sheet and spread it in an even layer—Bake it for about 35 minutes.
7. Remove from the oven and set aside to cool.
8. Add the chocolate pieces and stir to combine.
9. Enjoy.

Nutrition:

Calories - 193

Fat - 9.1 g

Carbs – 26.1 g

Protein – 5 g

Apple Pancakes

Preparation Time: 10 minutes

Cooking Time: 24 minutes

Servings: 6

Ingredients:

- ½ cup buckwheat flour
- 2 tbsp. coconut sugar *or Brown sugar*
- 1 tsp. Baking powder
- ½ tsp. ground cinnamon
- 1/3 cup unsweetened almond milk
- 1 egg, beaten lightly
- 2 granny smith apples, peeled, cored, and grated

Directions:

1. In a bowl, place the flour, coconut sugar, and cinnamon, and mix well.
2. In another bowl, place the almond milk and egg and beat until well combined.
3. Place the flour mixture and mix until well combined.
4. Fold in the grated apples.
5. Add the desired amount of mixture and, with a spoon, spread into an even layer.
6. Cook for 2 minutes on each side.
7. Repeat with the remaining mixture.
8. Serve warm with the drizzling of honey.

Nutrition:

Calories - 93

Fat - 2.1 g

Carbs – 22 g

Protein – 2.5 g

Breakfast Muesli

Preparation Time: 10 minutes

Cooking Time: 0 minutes

Servings: 2

Ingredients:

- ¾ oz. Buckwheat drops
- ⅜ oz. Buckwheat puffs
- ½ oz. coconut drops or dried up coconut
- 1 ½ oz. Medjool dates hollowed and slashed
- ½ oz. Pecans slashed
- ⅜ oz. cocoa nibs
- 3 ½ oz. strawberries, hulled and slashed
- 3 ½ oz. plain Greek yogurt

Directions:

1. In a blender, put all the listed ingredients.
2. Blend until smooth

3. Serve straight away.

Nutrition:

Calories - 334

Fat - 22.58 g

Carbs – 34.35 g

Protein – 4.39 g

Sirtfood Scrambled Eggs

Preparation Time: 15 minutes

Cooking Time: 7 minutes

Servings: 1

Ingredients:

- 1 tsp extra virgin olive oil
- ¾ oz. red onion, finely chopped
- ½ bird's eye chili, finely chopped
- 3 medium eggs
- 1.7 fl. oz. milk
- 1 tsp ground turmeric
- 3/16 oz. parsley, finely chopped

Directions:

1. In a skillet, heat the oil over high heat.
2. Toss in the red onion and chili, frying for 3 minutes.
3. In a large bowl, whisk together the milk, parsley, eggs, and turmeric.
4. Pour into the skillet and lower to medium heat.
5. Cook for 4 minutes, scrambling the mixture as you do with a spoon or spatula.
6. Serve immediately.

Nutrition:

Calories - 224

Fat - 14.63 g

Carbs – 4.79 g

Protein – 17.2 g

Strawberry Buckwheat Pancakes

Preparation Time: 5 minutes

Cooking Time: 6 minutes

Servings: 4

Ingredients:

- 3½ oz. strawberries, chopped
- 3½ oz. buckwheat flour
- 1 egg
- 8 fl oz. milk
- 1 tsp. olive oil
- 1 tsp. olive oil for frying
- Freshly squeezed juice of 1 orange

Directions:

1. Pour the milk into a bowl and mix in the egg and a tsp. of olive oil.
2. Sift in the flour to the liquid mixture until smooth and creamy.
3. Allow it to rest for 15 minutes.
4. Heat a little oil in a pan and pour in a quarter of the mixture or to the size you prefer.
5. Sprinkle in a quarter of the strawberries into the batter.
6. Cook for around 2 minutes on each side.
7. Serve hot with a drizzle of orange juice.

Nutrition:

Calories - 180

Fat - 7.5 g

Carbs – 22.58 g

Protein – 7.46 g

Blackcurrants Pancakes

Preparation Time: 5 minutes

Cooking Time: 50 minutes

Servings: 4

Ingredients:

- 2 apples, cut into small chunks
- 2 cups of quick-cooking oats

₂ 1 tsp cinnamon

- 1 cup flour of your choice
- 1 tsp baking powder
- 2 tbsp. honey
- 2 egg whites
- 1 ¼ cups of milk
- 2 tsp extra virgin olive oil
- A dash of salt
- For the berry topping:
- 1 cup blackcurrants, washed and stalks removed
- 3 tbsp. water
- 2 tbsp. honey

Directions:

1. Place the ingredients for the topping in a small pot simmer, frequently stirring for about 10 minutes until it cooks down and the juices are released.
2. Take the dry ingredients and mix them in a bowl. Afterward, add the apples and the milk a bit at a time you may not use it all) until it is a batter.
3. Stiffly whisk the egg whites and then gently mix them into the pancake batter. Set aside in the refrigerator.
4. Pour a one-quarter of the oil onto a flat pan or flat griddle, and when hot, pour some of the batter into it in a pancake shape.
5. When the pancakes start to have golden brown edges and form air bubbles, they may be ready to be gently flipped.
6. Repeat for the next three pancakes.
7. Top each pancake with the berries.

Nutrition:

Calories - 470

Fat - 16.83 g

Carbs – 79 g

Protein – 11.

71 g

Creamy Coconut Porridge

Preparation Time: 24 hours 20 minutes

Cooking Time: 5 minutes

Servings: 2

Ingredients:

- ¼ cup walnuts
- ½ cup Roasted Buckwheat Kernels
- 2 Medjool dates pitted
- 1 tbsp. chia seeds
- 1 tbsp. pure maple syrup
- 1 cup of coconut milk
- Pinch of salt

Directions:

1. In a large glass jar, soak the kasha and walnuts overnight.
2. Rinse the kasha and walnuts through a fine-mesh strainer under running water. Shaking the strainer several times, ensures thorough rinsing.
3. Place all the ingredients in a blender and blend for about 20 seconds.
4. Scrape down sides and blend again for another 10 seconds.
5. It can be served chilled or gently warmed.
6. Top with favourite toppings, and enjoy!

Nutrition:

Calories – 420

Fat - 28g

Carbs – 57g

Protein – 12g

Salmon & Kale Omelet

Preparation Time: 10 minutes

Cooking Time: 6 minutes

Servings: 4

Ingredients:

- 6 eggs

- 2 tbsp unsweetened almond milk
- Salt and black pepper, to taste
- 2 tbsp olive oil
- 4 oz. smoked salmon, cut into bite-sized chunks
- 2 cups fresh kale, tough ribs removed and chopped finely
- 4 scallions, chopped finely

Directions:

1. In a bowl, place the eggs, coconut milk, salt, and black pepper, and beat well then set aside.
2. In a non-stick wok, heat the oil over medium heat. Place the egg mixture and cook for about 30 seconds, without stirring.
3. Place the salmon kale and scallions on top of egg mixture evenly.
4. Reduce the heat to low.
5. With the lid, cover the wok and cook for about 4 minutes, or until omelet is done completely.
6. Uncover the wok and cook for about 1 minute.
7. Transfer the omelet onto a serving plate and serve.

Nutrition:

Calories 210

Fat 14.9 g

Carbs 5.2 g

Protein 14.8 g

Sirtfood Green Onion and Mushroom Omelet

Preparation Time: 10 minutes

Cooking Time: 5 minutes

Servings: 2

Ingredients:

- 6 oz. crimini mushrooms
- 2 tbsps. Plus 2 tsps. Butter

- 5 tbsps. Chopped green onions
- 1/4 cup dry vermouth
- 6 large eggs
- 1 tbsp. water
- 1/4 tsp. salt
- 1/4 tsp. ground black pepper

Directions:

1. In processor, finely chop mushrooms. Melt 2 tbsp. butter on medium high heat in medium skillet. Add 3 tbsp. onions and mushrooms; sauté for 3 minutes.
2. Add vermouth; boil for 1 1/2 minutes till evaporated. Season with pepper and salt.
3. Whisk pepper, salt, 1 tbsp. water and eggs to blend in medium bowl. Melt 1 tsp. butter on medium heat in small non-stick skillet.
4. Add 1/2 egg mixture; mix with back of a fork till edges start to set. Cook, lifting edges using a spatula so uncooked egg flows underneath, for 2 minutes till omelet is set.
5. Put 1/2 mushroom mixture down the middle of omelet then folds both omelet sides over fillingput onto plate.
6. Repeat using leftover mushroom mixture, egg mixture and butter. Sprinkle leftover onions on omelets.

Nutrition:

Calories per serving: 399

Carbohydrates: 15g

Protein: 1g

Fat: 0g

Sugar: 0.6g

Sodium: 506mg

Fiber: 1g

Lunch

Butternut pumpkin with buckwheat

Preparation Time: 5 Minutes

Cooking time: 50 Minutes

Servings: 4

Ingredients:

- One tablespoon of extra virgin olive oil
- One red onion, finely chopped
- One tablespoon fresh ginger, finely chopped
- Three cloves of garlic, finely chopped
- Two small chilies, finely chopped
- One tablespoon cumin
- One cinnamon stick
- Two tablespoons turmeric
- 800g chopped canned tomatoes
- 300ml vegetable broth
- 100g dates, seeded and chopped
- one 400g tin of chickpeas, drained
- 500g butter squash, peeled, seeded and cut into pieces
- 200g buckwheat
- 5g coriander, chopped
- 10g parsley, chopped

Directions:

1. Preheat the oven to 400 °.
2. Heat the olive oil in a frying pan and sauté the onion, ginger, garlic, and Thai chili. After two minutes, add cumin, cinnamon, and turmeric and cook for another two minutes while stirring.
3. Add the tomatoes, dates, stock, and chickpeas, stir well and cook over low heat for 45 to 60 minutes. Add some water as required. In the meantime, mix the pumpkin pieces with olive oil. Bake in the oven for about 30 minutes until soft.
4. Cook the buckwheat according to the directions and add the remaining turmeric. When everything is cooked, add the pumpkin to the other ingredients in the roaster and serve with the buckwheat. Sprinkle with coriander and parsley.

Nutrition:

Calories per serving 248.1

Total Fat .8.7g

Saturated fat per serving 2.6g

Monounsaturated fat per serving 1.5g

Polyunsaturated fat per serving 4.0g

Protein per serving 8.5g

Roasted Artichoke Hearts

Preparation Time: 5 minutes

Cooking Time: 40 minutes

Servings: 3

Ingredients:

- 2 cans artichoke hearts
- 4 garlic cloves, quartered
- 2 tsp extra virgin olive oil
- 1 tsp dried oregano
- salt and pepper, to taste
- 2-3 tbsp lemon juice, to serve

Directions:

1. Preheat oven to 375F.
2. Drain the artichoke hearts and rinse them very thoroughly.
3. Toss them in garlic, oregano, and olive oil.
4. Arrange the artichoke hearts in a baking dish and bake for about 45 minutes tossing a few times if desired.
5. Season with salt and pepper and serve with lemon juice.

Nutrition:

Calories: 35

Fat: 20 g

Carbohydrates: 3 g

Protein: 1 g

Fiber: 1 g

Beef Broth

Preparation Time: 5 minutes

Cooking Time: 40 minutes

Servings: 3

Ingredients:

- 4-5 pounds beef bones and few veal bones
- 1 pound of stew meat (chuck or flank steak) cut into 2-inch chunks
- Olive oil
- 1-2 medium red onions, peeled and quartered
- 1-2 large carrots, cut into 1-2-inch segments
- 1 celery rib, cut into 1-inch segments
- 2-3 cloves of garlic, unpeeled
- A handful of parsley stems and leaves
- 1-2 bay leaves
- 10 peppercorns

Directions:

1. Heat oven to 375F.
2. Rub olive oil over the stew meat pieces, carrots, and onions.
3. Put stew meat or beef scraps, stock bones, carrots, and onions in a large roasting pan.
4. Roast in the oven for about 45 minutes, turning everything halfway through the cooking.
5. Place everything from the oven in a large stockpot.
6. Pour some boiling water in the oven pan and scrape up all the browned bits and pour all in the stockpot.
7. Add parsley, celery, garlic, bay leaves, and peppercorns to the pot.
8. Fill the pot with cold water, to 1-inch over the top of the bones.
9. Bring the stockpot to a regular simmer and then reduce the heat to low, so it just barely simmers. Cover the pot loosely and let simmer low and slow for 3-4 hours.
10. Scoop away the fat and any scum that rises to the surface occasionally.
11. After cooking, remove the bones and vegetables from the pot.
12. Strain the broth.
13. Let cool to room temperature and then put in the refrigerator.
14. The fat will solidify once the broth has chilled.
15. Discard the fat (or reuse it) and pour the broth into a jar and freeze it.

Nutrition:

Calories: 65

Fat: 1 g

Carbohydrates: 2 g

Protein: 3 g

Fiber: 0 g

Salmon and Capers

Preparation Time: 5 minutes

Cooking Time: 40 minutes

Servings: 3

Ingredients:

- 75g (3oz) Greek yoghurt
- 4 salmon fillets, skin removed
- 4 tsp Dijon mustard
- 1 tbsp capers, chopped
- 2 tsp fresh parsley
- Zest of 1 lemon

Directions:

1. In a bowl, mix the yoghurt, mustard, lemon zest, parsley, and capers.
2. Thoroughly coat the salmon in the mixture.

3. Place the salmon under a hot grill (broiler) and cook for 3-4 minutes on each side, or until the fish is cooked.
4. Serve with mashed potatoes and vegetables or a large green leafy salad.

Nutrition:

Calories: 283

Fat: 25 g

Carbohydrates: 1 g

Protein: 20 g

Fiber: 0 g

Pasta Salad

Preparation Time: 5 minutes

Cooking Time: 40 minutes

Servings: 3

- **Ingredients:**
- A plate of mixed greens ingredients
- 1 box (16 ounces) elbow pasta
- 4 cups of water
- 1 tbsp fit salt
- 2 tbsp olive oil
- ½ cup red onion, diced
- 1 cup simmered red peppers, daintily cut
- ¼ cup dark olives, cut
- ½ pound (8 ounces) crisp mozzarella, diced
- ½ cup slashed basil
- Red wine vinaigrette ingredients
- 1 box (16 ounces) elbow pasta
- 4 cups of water
- 1 tbsp fit salt
- 2 tbsp olive oil
- ½ cup red onion, diced
- 1 cup simmered red peppers, daintily cut
- ¼ cup dark olives, cut
- ½ pound (8 ounces) crisp mozzarella, diced

[handwritten: ¼C O O. 1 tsp RWV added cherry 12 tomatos]

- ½ cup slashed basil

Directions:

1. Amass pressure top, ensuring the weight discharge valve is in the seal position.
2. Select pressure and set it to high. Set time to 3 minutes.
3. Select start/stop to start.
4. While the pasta is cooking, set up the red wine vinaigrette.
5. In a blending bowl, join all vinaigrette fixings aside from olive oil.
6. Gradually speed in the olive oil until wholly joined.
7. Taste and alter seasonings as wanted.
8. Put in a safe spot.
9. At the point when weight cooking is finished, enable the strain to discharge for 10 minutes regularly.
10. Following 10 minutes, snappy discharge remaining weight by moving the weight discharge valve to the vent position.
11. Cautiously expel top when the unit has completed the process of discharging pressure.
12. Evacuate the pot and strain the pasta in a colander.
13. Move to a bowl and hurl with 2 tbsp of olive oil.
14. Spot bowl in cooler and enable pasta to cool for 20 minutes.
15. When pasta has cooled, mix in red onion, broiled peppers, dark olives, mozzarella, and basil.
16. Delicately crease in the red wine vinaigrette.
17. Serve quickly or cover and refrigerate for serving later.

Nutrition:

Calories: 248

Fat: 6 g

Carbohydrates: 36 g

Protein: 9 g

Fiber: 0 g

Sirtfood Caramel Coated Catfish

Preparation time: 15 minutes

Cooking time: 45 minutes

Serving: 4

Ingredients:

- 1/3 cup water
- 2 tbsps. Fish sauce
- 2 shallots, chopped
- 4 cloves garlic, minced
- 1 1/2 tsps. Ground black pepper
- 1/4 tsp. red pepper flakes
- 1/3 cup water
- 1/3 cup white sugar
- 2 lbs. catfish fillets
- 1/2 tsp. white sugar
- 1 tbsp. fresh lime juice
- 1 green onion, thinly sliced
- 1/2 cup chopped cilantro

Directions:

1. Combine fish sauce and 1/3 cup of water in a small bowl; mix and put aside.
2. Combine together shallots, red pepper flakes, black pepper and garlic in another bowl and put aside.
3. Heat 1/3 cup of sugar and 1/3 cup of water in a big skillet placed over medium heat, stirring from time to time until sugar becomes deep golden brown. Stir in the fish sauce mixture gently and let the mixture boil. Mix and cook the shallot mixture.
4. Once the shallots have softened, add the catfish to the mixture.
5. Cook the catfish with cover for about 5 minutes each side until the fish can be easily flake using a fork. Transfer the catfish to a large plate, place a cover,

and put aside. Adjust the heat to high and mix in a half tsp. of sugar.
6. Stir in any sauce that left on the plate and the lime juice.
7. Let it boil and simmer until the sauce has cooked down.
8. Drizzle the sauce on top of the catfish and sprinkle with cilantro and green onions.

Nutrition:

Calories per serving: 254

Carbohydrates: 4g

Protein: 1g

Fat: 0.5g

Sugar: 3g

Sodium: 96mg

Fiber: 1g

Lentil Tacos

Preparation time: 10 minutes

Cooking time: 12 minutes

Servings: 8

Ingredients:

- 2 cups cooked lentils
- ½ cup chopped green bell pepper
- ½ cup chopped white onion
- ½ cup halved grape tomatoes
- 1 teaspoon minced garlic
- ½ teaspoon garlic powder
- 1 teaspoon red chili powder
- ½ teaspoon smoked paprika
- ½ teaspoon ground cumin
- 8 whole-grain tortillas

Directions:

1. Take a large skillet pan, place it over medium heat, add oil, and let it heat.
2. Add onion, bell pepper, and garlic, stir until mixed, and then cook for 5 minutes until vegetables begin to soften.

3. Add lentils and tomatoes, stir in all the spices and then continue cooking for 5 minutes until hot.
4. Assemble the tacos and for this, heat the tortillas until warmed and then fill each tortilla with ¼ cup of the cooked lentil mixture.
5. Serve straight away.

Nutrition:

Calories: 315

Fat: 7.8 g

Protein: 13 g

Carbs: 49.8 g

Fiber: 16.2 g

Lentil and Quinoa Salad

Preparation time: 5 minutes

Cooking time: 15 minutes

Servings: 4

Ingredients:

*   2 medium green apples, cored, chopped
*   3 cups cooked quinoa
*   ½ of a medium red onion, peeled, diced
*   3 cups cooked green lentils
*   1 large carrot, shredded
*   1 ½ teaspoon salt
*   1 teaspoon ground black pepper
*   2 tablespoons olive oil
*   ¼ cup balsamic vinegar

Directions:

1. Take a large bowl, place all the ingredients in it and then stir until combined.
2. Let the salad chill in the refrigerator for 1 hour, divide it evenly among six bowls and then serve.

Nutrition:

Calories: 199

Fat: 10.7 g

Protein: 8 g

Carbs: 34.8 g

Fiber: 5.9 g

Sloppy Joes

Preparation time: 5 minutes

Cooking time: 15 minutes

Servings: 4

Ingredients:

*   2 cups cooked lentils
*   2/3 cup diced white onion
*   1 medium sweet potato, peeled, chopped
*   1 medium red bell pepper, cored, diced
*   1 teaspoon minced garlic
*   ¾ cup chopped mushrooms
*   1 teaspoon red chili powder
*   1 teaspoon paprika
*   1 teaspoon ground cumin
*   1 tablespoon brown sugar
*   1 tablespoon Worcestershire sauce
*   1 tablespoon olive oil
*   ½ cup vegetable broth
*   15 ounces tomato sauce

Directions:

1. Take a large pan, place it over medium-high heat, add oil, and then let it heat.
2. Add onion, bell pepper, garlic, mushroom, and sweet potato, stir until mixed, and then cook for 8 minutes or more until potatoes turn tender.
3. Add lentils, stir in sugar and all the spices, pour in the tomato sauce and then cook for 3 minutes until thoroughly hot.
4. Pour in the broth, bring the mixture to a simmer, and then remove the pan from heat.
5. Ladle the sloppy Joes mixture over the bun and then serve.

Nutrition:

Calories: 125.3

Fat: 3.6 g

Protein: 2.8 g

Carbs: 20.1 g

Fiber: 3 g

Lentil Burgers

Preparation time: 10 minutes

Cooking time: 10 minutes

Servings: 4

Ingredients:

- 2 cups cooked green lentils
- 2 tablespoons chopped white onion
- 4 ounces sliced mushrooms
- 1 teaspoon minced garlic
- 2 teaspoons garlic powder
- 2/3 teaspoon salt
- ½ teaspoon ground black pepper
- 1 tablespoon Worcestershire sauce
- 1 tablespoon yellow mustard
- 2 tablespoons olive oil
- 5 hamburger buns

Directions:

1. Place the cooked lentils in a blender, pulse until blended, and then tip the mixture into a medium bowl, set aside until required.
2. Place 1 tablespoon oil in a medium skillet pan, place it over medium heat, and when hot, add onion, mushrooms, and garlic.
3. Cook for 3 minutes, spoon the mixture to a food processor, add mustard, Worcestershire sauce, and 1 bun, and then pulse until slightly smooth.
4. Tip the mushroom mixture to lentil, and then stir until combined.

5. Add salt, black pepper, and garlic powder, stir until mixed, and then shape the mixture into four patties.
6. Place a skillet pan over medium heat, add remaining oil and when hot, add patties and then cook for 3 minutes per side until golden brown.
7. Arrange the patty on a bun and then serve with favorite condiments.

Nutrition:

Calories: 184

Fat: 4 g

Protein: 11 g

Carbs: 28 g

Fiber: 9 g

Potato Salad

Preparation time: 5 minutes

Cooking time: 25 minutes

Servings: 4

Ingredients:

- 2 medium potatoes
- 2 medium tomatoes, diced
- 2 celery, diced
- 1 green onion, chopped

Directions:

1. Place the potatoes into a pan, cover with water, and then place the pan over medium-high heat.
2. Cook the potatoes for 20 minutes, and when done, drain them and let them cool.
3. Peel the potatoes, cut them into cubes, and then place them into a large bowl.
4. Add tomatoes, celery, and green onion, season with salt and black pepper, drizzle with oil and then toss until coated.
5. Divide the salad between three bowls and then serve.

Nutrition:

Calories: 268.5

Fat: 15.8 g

Protein: 5 g

Carbs: 21 g

Fiber: 2.5 g

Ginger Brown Rice

Preparation time: 5 minutes

Cooking time: 40 minutes

Servings: 3

Ingredients:

- 1 cup brown rice, rinsed
- 1-inch grated ginger
- ½ of Serrano pepper, chopped
- 1 green onion, chopped
- 2 cups of water

Directions:

1. Take a medium pot, place it over medium-high heat, and then pour in water.
2. Add rice, green onion, Serrano pepper, and ginger, bring to a boil, switch heat to medium and then simmer for 30 minutes.
3. Divide rice among three bowls and then serve.

Nutrition:

Calories: 125

Fat: 1 g

Protein: 3 g

Carbs: 26 g

Fiber: 0 g

Pasta with kale and Black Olive

Preparation time: 10 minutes

Cooking time: 40 minutes

Servings: 3

Ingredients:

- 60 g of buckwheat pasta
- 180 gr of pasta
- Six leaves of washed curly kale
- 20 black olives
- Two tablespoons of oil
- ½ chili pepper

Directions:

1. Cut the curly kale leaves into strips about 4 cm wide; cook them in salted boiling water for 5 minutes. Also, add the pasta to the pan. While the pasta is cooking, in a nonstick pan, towards the oil and olives. Drain the pasta and cabbage (keeping some cooking water aside) and add them to the olives. Mix well, adding, if needed, a little cooking water. Add the chili pepper and keep everything well.

Nutrition:

Calories per serving 372.7

Total Fat .28.0g

Saturated fat per serving 2.7g

Monounsaturated fat per serving 10.0g

Polyunsaturated fat per serving 2.1g

Protein per serving 3.6g

Dinner

Tofu Thai Curry

Preparation Time: 5 Minutes

Cooking time: 65 Minutes

Servings: 2

Ingredients:

- 400g (14oz) tofu, diced
- 200g (7oz) sugar snaps peas
- 5cm (2 inches) chunk fresh ginger root, peeled and finely chopped

- 2 red onions, chopped
- 2 cloves of garlic, crushed
- 2 bird's eye chilies
- 2 tablespoons tomato puree
- 1 stalk of lemongrass, inner stalks only
- 1 tablespoon fresh coriander (cilantro), chopped
- 1 teaspoon cumin
- 300mls (½ pint) coconut milk
- 200mls (7fl oz) vegetable stock (broth)
- 1 tablespoon virgin olive oil
- Juice of 1 lime

Directions:

2. Heat the oil in a frying pan, add the onion and cook for 4 minutes. Add in the chilies, cumin, ginger, and garlic and cook for 2 minutes. Add the tomato puree, lemongrass, sugar-snap peas, lime juice, and tofu and cook for 2 minutes. Pour in the stock (broth), coconut milk and coriander (cilantro) and simmer for 5 minutes. Serve with brown rice or buckwheat and a handful of rockets (arugula) leaves on the side.

Nutrition:

Calories 346.3

Total fat 26.4 g

Saturated fat Trace 2.0 g

Trans fat 0 g

Monounsaturated fat 5.4 g

Cholesterol Trace. 0.0 mg

Beef bourguignon with Mashed potatoes and kale

Preparation time: 15 minutes

Cooking time: 2 - 3 hours

Serving: 4

Ingredients:

- 800 g diced beef
- 2–3 tbsp buckwheat flour
- 1 tbsp extra virgin olive oil
- 150 g red onion, roughly chopped
- 200 g celery, roughly chopped
- 100 g carrots, roughly chopped
- 2–3 cloves of garlic, chopped
- 375 ml of red wine
- 2 tbsp tomato puree
- 750 ml beef broth
- 2 bay leaves
- 1 sprig of fresh thyme or 1 tablespoon of dried thyme
- 75 g diced pancetta or smoked lard
- 250 g mushrooms
- 2 tbsp chopped parsley
- 200 g kale
- 1 tbsp corn flour or arrowroot (optional)
- For the porridge:
- 500g Edward potatoes
- 1 tbsp milk and 1 tbsp olive oil

Directions:

3. Pat the beef dry with kitchen paper. Heat a heavy saucepan over medium-high heat. Add the olive oil, then the beef and saute the meat until it is browned nicely all over. Depending on the size of your pan, it's best to do this in 3-4 small loads.

4. When all of the meat is brown, remove it from the pan with a slotted spoon and set aside. In the same pan, add the onion, celery, carrot and garlic and fry over medium heat for 3 to 4 minutes until tender. Add the wine, tomato paste and broth and bring to a boil. Add the browned beef, bay leaves and thyme and reduce the heat to a simmer. Cover the pan with a lid and cook for 2 hours, stirring from time to time to make sure nothing sticks to the bottom. While the beef is cooking, peel your potatoes and cut them into quarters (or smaller pieces if they're quite large).

5. Put in a pan with cold water and bring to a boil. Reduce the heat to a simmer and cook for 20-25 minutes, covered with a lid. When soft, drain and mash with olive oil and milk. Keep warm. While the potatoes are boiling, heat a pan over high heat. When it's hot but not smoking, add the diced pancetta.

6. The fat content of the bacon means you don't need oil to cook it. When some of the fat has been released and it's starting to brown, add the mushrooms and cook over medium heat until both are nicely browned. Depending on the size of your pan, you may need to do this in multiple loads. Set aside after cooking. Cook or steam the kale for 5–10 minutes until soft. Once the beef is tender enough and the sauce has thickened to your liking, add the pancetta, mushrooms, and parsley. If your sauce is still a little runny, you can mix the corn flour or arrowroot with a little water and then stir the paste into the sauce until you have the consistency you want. Cook for 2-3 minutes and serve with porridge and kale.

Nutrition:

Carbohydrates: 34

Fat: 25

Protein: 31

Kcal: 510

Turkish fajitas

Preparation time: 15 minutes

Cooking time: approx. 1 hour

Serving: 4

Ingredients:

- For the filling
- Cut 500 g turkey breast into strips
- 1 tablespoon of extra virgin olive oil 1-2 chilies, depending on taste, chopped
- 150 g red onion, thinly sliced
- 150 g red pepper, cut into thin strips
- 2–3 cloves of garlic, chopped
- 1 tbsp paprika
- 1 tbsp ground cumin
- 1 teaspoon chili powder
- 1 tbsp chopped coriander
- For the guacamole
- 2 ripe avocados, peeled (reserve one of the stones)
- Juice of 1 lime
- Pinch of chili powder
- Pinch of black pepper
- For the salsa
- 1 × 400 g can of chopped tomatoes
- 20 g red onion, diced
- 20 g red pepper, deseeded and diced
- Juice of ½ - 1 lime, depending on the size
- 1 teaspoon chopped coriander
- 1 teaspoon capers

For the salad

- 100 g rocket
- 3 tomatoes, cut
- 100 g cucumber, thinly sliced
- 1 tbsp extra virgin olive oil juice of ½ lemon
- For serving
- 100 g cheddar cheese
- 8 grated whole grain tortilla wraps

Directions:

1. Mix the filling ingredients together and set them aside while you prepare the other parts.

2. Put all of the guacamole ingredients in a small food processor and flash until a smooth paste is formed. Alternatively, you can mash them all together with the back of a fork or spoon.

3. Place the reserved avocado stone in the guacamole - it will keep it from turning

brown. Mix all the ingredients for the salsa.

4. Put all the salad ingredients in a large bowl. Put your largest pan on high heat until it starts to smoke.
5. Put the turkey filling in the hot pan - you may need to cook it in 2 to 3 loads as overcrowding the pan will create too much moisture and it will start boiling instead of frying.
6. Keep the pan over high heat and keep moving the mixture so the turkey colors nicely but doesn't burn.
7. In a low oven, keep the cooked meat warm. To serve, reheat the tortillas according to the directions in the package, then sprinkle some guacamole over each package.
8. Top with some cheese and some salsa, then stack the turkey mixture in the middle and roll it up like a large cigar. Serve with the salad.

Nutrition:

Carbohydrates: 44

Fat: 21

Protein: 30

Kcal: 450

Sirt Chicken Korma

Preparation time: 10 minutes

Cooking time: 50 minutes

Serving: 4

Ingredients:

- 350 ml chicken stock
- 30 g Medjool date, chopped
- 2 cinnamon sticks
- 4–5 cardamom pods, slightly split
- 250 ml coconut milk
- 8 boneless, skinless chicken thighs
- 1 tbsp ground turmeric
- 200 g buckwheat
- 150 ml of Greek yogurt
- 50 g of ground walnuts
- 2 tbsp chopped coriander

For the curry paste

- 1 large red onion, quartered
- 3 cloves of garlic
- 2 cm piece of fresh ginger
- 1 tbsp mild curry powder
- 1 teaspoon ground cumin
- 1 tbsp ground turmeric
- 1 tbsp coconut oil

Directions:

1. Put the ingredients for the curry paste in a food processor and flash for about a minute until you have a nice paste.
2. Alternatively, you can grind it with a pestle and mortar. Fry the paste in a heavy pan over medium heat for 1-2 minutes then add the broth, date, cinnamon, cardamom pods, and coconut milk.
3. Bring to a boil then add the chicken legs. Reduce the heat, cover the pan with a lid, and simmer for 45 minutes.
4. In the meantime, bring a pan of water to the boil and stir in the turmeric.
5. Add the buckwheat and cook according to the directions on the package. As soon as the chicken is tender, stir in the yogurt and cook the walnuts over low heat for a few more minutes.
6. Add the coriander and serve with the buckwheat

Nutrition:

Carbohydrates: 21

Fat: 16

Protein: 32

Kcal: 330

Tomato Chicken Mix

Preparation Time: 10 minutes

Cooking Time: 20 minutes

Serve: 6

Ingredients:

- 14 ounces tomato sauce
- 1 tablespoon olive oil
- 4 medium chicken breasts, skinless and boneless
- Salt and black pepper to taste
- 1 teaspoon oregano, dried
- 6 ounces mozzarella cheese, grated
- 1 teaspoon garlic powder

Directions:

1. Put the chicken in your air fryer and season with salt, pepper, garlic powder, and the oregano.
2. Cook the chicken at 360 degrees F for 5 minutes; then transfer to a pan that fits your air fryer, greased with the oil.
3. Add the tomato sauce, sprinkle the mozzarella on top, place the pan in the fryer, and cook at 350 degrees F for 15 minutes more.
4. Divide between plates and serve.

Nutrition:

calories 270

fat 10

fiber 16

carbs 16

protein 18

Chicken and Veggies

Preparation Time: 10 minutes

Cooking Time: 25 minutes

Serve: 4

Ingredients:

- 1 red onion, chopped
- 1 carrot, chopped
- 3 garlic cloves, minced
- 4 chicken breasts, boneless and skinless
- 1 celery stalk, chopped
- 1 cup chicken stock
- 2 tablespoons olive oil
- ½ teaspoon rosemary, dried
- 1 teaspoon sage, dried
- Salt and black pepper to taste

Directions:

1. In a pan that fits your air fryer, place all ingredients and toss well.
2. Put the pan in the fryer and cook at 360 degrees F for 25 minutes.
3. Divide everything between plates, serve, and enjoy!

Nutrition:

calories 292

fat 12

fiber 16

carbs 19

protein 15

Japanese Chicken Thighs

Preparation Time: 10 minutes

Cooking Time: 30 minutes

Serve: 5

Ingredients:

- 2 pounds chicken thighs
- Salt and black pepper to taste
- 5 spring onions, chopped
- 2 tablespoons olive oil
- 1 tablespoon sherry wine
- ½ teaspoon white vinegar
- 1 tablespoon soy sauce
- ¼ teaspoon sugar

Directions:

1. Season the chicken with salt and pepper, rub with 1 tablespoon of the oil, and put it in the air fryer's basket.
2. Cook at 360 degrees F for 10 minutes on each side and divide between plates.
3. Heat up a pan with the remaining tablespoon of oil over medium-high heat, and add the spring onions, sherry wine, vinegar, soy sauce, and sugar; whisk.
4. Cook for 10 minutes, drizzle over the chicken, and serve.

Nutrition:

calories 271

fat 8

fiber 12

carbs 26

protein 17

Air Fried Whole Chicken

Preparation Time: 10 minutes

Cooking Time: 20 minutes

Serve: 8

Ingredients:

- 1 whole chicken, cut into medium pieces
- 3 tablespoons white wine
- 2 carrots, chopped
- 1 cup chicken stock
- 1 tablespoon ginger, grated
- Salt and black pepper to taste

Directions:

1. In a pan that fits your air fryer, mix all of the ingredients.
2. Put the pan in the air fryer and cook at 370 degrees F for 20 minutes.
3. Divide between plates and serve.

Nutrition:

calories 220

fat 10

fiber 8

carbs 20

protein 16

Perfect Garlic Butter Steak

Preparation Time: 20 minutes

Cooking Time: 13 minutes

Serve: 4

Ingredients:

- 2 Rib eye steaks
- Salt
- Pepper
- Olive oil
- Garlic butter:
- ½ cup softened butter
- 2 tbsp chopped fresh parsley
- 2 garlic cloves, minced
- 1 tsp Worcestershire sauce
- ½ tsp salt (optional)

Directions:

1. Prepare the garlic butter by mixing all the ingredients together.
2. Place in parchment paper. Roll up and put in the fridge.
3. Let the steaks sit for 20 minutes at room temperature.
4. Brush with a little oil, salt, and pepper.
5. Preheat your hot air fryer to 400°F (200°C).
6. Cook for 12 minutes, turning halfway through cooking. Serve.
7. Place the garlic butter on the steaks and let sit for 5 minutes.
8. Enjoy!

Nutrition:

Calories 250

Fat 10g

Carbohydrates 2g

Sugars 1g

Protein 36g

Cholesterol 100mg

Crispy Pork Medallions

Preparation time: 20 minutes

Cooking time: 5 minutes

Serve: 2

Ingredients:

- 1 pork loin, 330 g, cut into 6 or 7 slices of 4 cm
- 1 tsp Dijon mustard
- 1 tsp oil
- Salt, pepper and paprika
- Asian marinade
- 1 tsp salt reduced tamari sauce
- 1 tsp olive oil
- 1 clementine juice
- 1 pinch cayenne pepper
- 2 cloves garlic, pressed
- Crunchy coating
- 1/3 cup breadcrumbs
- ½ orange zest
- 2g freshly grated Parmesan cheese

Direction:

1. Prepare the marinade first. In a bowl, combine all the ingredients. Lightly salt the medallions, pepper, and sprinkle with paprika. Place these in the marinade and turn them several times to impregnate them completely. Cover with plastic wrap and marinate for 1 hour at room temperature.
2. Prepare the coating by combining the breadcrumbs, the orange zest, and the Parmesan cheese in a deep dish.
3. When the maceration time has elapsed, remove the marinade medallions, and dry them on absorbent paper. Spread with mustard, then move on to the crunchy layer. Brush lightly with oil.

4. Heat the air fryer to 350°F. Place the medallions in the fryer basket. Cook 5 minutes, stir, and then return to the fryer for another minute. Serve immediately.

Nutrition:

Calories 222

Carbohydrates 13g

Fat 6g

Protein 24g

Sugars 0h

Cholesterol 74mg

Prawns, Pak Choi and broccoli

Preparation time: 15 minutes

Cooking time: 20 minutes

Serving: 5

Ingredients:

- 1 tbsp ground turmeric
- 400 g raw shrimp, peeled and deveined
- 1 tbsp coconut oil
- 280 g buckwheat noodles
- 1 teaspoon virgin olive oil
- For the china pan
- 1 tbsp coconut oil
- Cut 250 g broccoli into bite-sized pieces
- 250 g pak choi, roughly chopped
- 1 red onion, thinly sliced
- 2 cm piece of fresh ginger, chopped
- 1–2 chili peppers, chopped
- 3 cloves of garlic, chopped
- 150 ml vegetable broth
- 1 bunch of basil, removed leaves and chopped stems
- 1 tbsp Thai fish sauce or tamari

Directions:

1. Mix the turmeric with the prawns. Place the coconut oil in a wok or pan and cook the shrimp over medium-high heat for 3 to 4 minutes, or until opaque.

2. After cooking, remove from pan and set aside. Wipe the pan for the pan and put it on high heat until it starts to smoke.
3. Add the coconut oil then add the vegetables, ginger, chili peppers, and garlic.
4. Keep moving the vegetables in the pan so they don't burn. Cook for 3–5 minutes - lower the heat a little if the vegetables look charred - until they are fried but crispy.
5. Add the broth, whole basil and fish sauce.
6. Bring to the boil, then add the shrimp and let heat. In the meantime, cook the pasta according to the instructions on the package.
7. Freshen up in cold water and mix with the olive oil to prevent them from sticking together. Serve the pan with the hot noodles.

Nutrition:

Carbohydrates: 13

Fat: 15

Protein: 26

Kcal: 270

Cocoa spaghetti Bolognese

Preparation time: 15 minutes

Cooking time: approx. 1 hour

Serving: 4

Ingredients:

- 1 tbsp virgin olive oil
- 1 red onion, finely diced
- 100 g celery, finely diced
- 100 g carrots, finely diced
- 3 cloves of garlic, chopped
- 400 g of lean ground beef
- 1 tbsp Herbs de Provence
- 1–2 bay leaves
- 150 ml red wine
- 300 ml beef broth

- 1 tbsp cocoa powder
- 1 tbsp tomato paste
- 2 × 400 g cans of chopped tomatoes
- 280 g whole wheat spaghetti
- 1 teaspoon ground black pepper
- 1 bunch of fresh basil
- 20 g parmesan cheese

Directions:

1. Heat the oil in a pan, then cook the onion, celery, carrot and garlic over medium heat for 1–2 minutes until they are a little softer.
2. Add the ground beef and dried herbs and cook over medium-high heat until the ground beef is brown.
3. Add the wine, stock, cocoa powder, tomato paste and canned tomatoes, bring to a boil and simmer for 45 to 60 minutes with the lid closed.
4. When you're almost done, cook the pasta as directed on the package.
5. Finally stir the pepper and basil leaves into the sauce. Serve with the pasta and rub some parmesan on top.

Nutrition:

Carbohydrates: 43

Fat: 21

Protein: 11

Kcal: 450

Baked salmon with Watercress sauce and Potatoes

Preparation time: 10 minutes

Cooking time: 35 minutes

Serving: 4

Ingredients:

- 400 g of new potatoes
- 4 × 125 g skinless salmon fillets
- 1 teaspoon extra virgin olive oil
- 1 piece of broccoli, cut into florets

- 1 bunch of asparagus spears
- For the watercress sauce
- 30 g of watercress
- 5 g parsley
- 1 tbsp capers
- 2 tbsp virgin olive oil
- Extra juice of 1 lemon

Directions:

1. Heat the oven to 200 ° C / gas. 6. Put the potatoes in a pan with cold water.
2. Bring to a boil and simmer for 15-20 minutes or until tender.
3. Brush the salmon fillets with the olive oil, place on a baking sheet and bake in the oven for 10 minutes.
4. Reduce the cooking time by 2 to 3 minutes if you prefer your salmon to be lightly cooked.
5. In the meantime, cook or steam the broccoli and asparagus until tender.
6. Put the ingredients for the sauce in a food processor or blender and stir until smooth. Serve the salmon with the sauce and the vegetables.

Nutrition:

Carbohydrates: 9

Fat: 15

Protein: 31

Kcal: 250

Coq au vin with potatoes and green beans

Preparation time: 10 minutes

Cooking time: 35 minutes

Serving: 4

Ingredients:

- 4 skinless chicken legs
- 4 skinless chicken legs
- 1-2 tbsp buckwheat flour
- 1 tbsp extra virgin olive oil

- 150 g red onion
- 150 g carrot
- 200 g celery
- 3 cloves of garlic, chopped
- 400 ml red wine
- 400 ml of chicken broth
- 1 sprig of fresh thyme
- 2–3 bay leaves
- 100 g pancetta or smoked bacon, diced
- 250 g mushrooms
- 400 g of new potatoes
- 2 tbsp chopped parsley
- 250 g green beans

Directions:

1. Roll the chicken pieces in the flour. Heat a heavy saucepan over medium-high heat. Add the olive oil then the chicken and cook until nicely browned all over.
2. Remove from pan and set aside. In the same pan, add the onion, carrot, celery and garlic and cook gently for 2-3 minutes until they soften.
3. When the pan is dry, you can add some water here. Add the wine and chicken stock and bring to a boil. Add the thyme, bay leaves, and chicken. Cover with a lid and simmer gently for 45 minutes.
4. Check the amount of fluid from time to time and add a little more. Heat a pan over high heat. When it's hot but not smoking, add the diced pancetta.
5. When some of the fat has been released and it starts to brown, add the mushrooms and cook over medium heat until both it and the pancetta are nicely browned.
6. Depending on the size of your pan, you may need to do this in multiple loads. Set aside after cooking.
7. Put the potatoes in a pan with cold water. Bring to a boil and simmer for 15-20 minutes or until tender. When you're

done, drain it and return to the pan to keep it warm.

8. Add the pancetta, mushrooms and parsley to the Coq au Vin and cook for another 15 minutes.
9. To cook the green beans, steam them or cook them for 4 to 6 minutes, depending on how crispy you like them.
10. Serve the Coq au Vin with the potatoes and beans.

Nutrition:

Carbohydrates: 13

Fat: 15

Protein: 26

Kcal: 270

Beans & Kale Soup

Preparation Time: 15 minutes

Cooking Time: 30 minutes

Servings: 6

Ingredients:

- 2 tablespoons olive oil
- 2 onions, chopped
- 4 garlic cloves, minced
- 1-pound kale, tough ribs removed and chopped
- 2 (14-ounce) cans cannellini beans, rinsed and drained
- 6 cups of water
- Salt and ground black pepper, as required

Directions:

1. In a large pan, heat the oil over medium heat and sauté the onion and garlic for about 4-5 minutes.
2. Add the kale and cook for about 1-2 minutes.
3. Add beans, water, salt, and black pepper and bring to a boil.

4. Cook partially covered for about 15-20 minutes.
5. Serve hot.

Nutrition:

Calories 270.4.

Total fat 4.7 g.

Saturated fat Trace 0.6 g.

Trans fat 0 g.

Monounsaturated fat 2.6 g.

Cholesterol Trace. 0.0 mg

Salad

Orange & Beet Salad

Preparation Time: 15 minutes

Servings: 4

Ingredients:

- 3 large oranges, peeled, seeded and sectioned
- 2 beets, trimmed, peeled and sliced
- 6 cups fresh rocket
- ¼ cup walnuts, chopped
- 3 tablespoons olive oil
- Pinch of salt

Directions:

1. In a salad bowl, place all ingredients and gently, toss to coat.
2. Serve immediately.

Nutrition:

Calories 233

Total Fat 15.6 g

Saturated Fat 1.8 g

Cholesterol 0 mg

Sodium 86 mg

Total Carbs 23.1 g

Fiber 5.3 g

Sugar 17.6 g

Protein 4.8 g

Faro Salad with White Beans

Preparation time: 30 minutes

Cooking time: 32 minutes

Servings: 4

Ingredients:

- 12 ounces (340 g) sugar snap peas, strings removed and cut into 1-inch lengths
- 3¼ teaspoon sea salt, plus more to taste, divided (optional)
- 1½ cups whole faro
- 3 tablespoons extra-virgin olive oil (optional)
- 2 tablespoons lemon juice
- 2 tablespoons minced shallot
- 1 teaspoon Dijon mustard
- ¼ teaspoon black pepper, plus more to taste, divided
- 1 (15-ounce / 425-g) can cannellini beans, rinsed
- 6 ounces (170 g) cherry tomatoes, halved
- ⅓ cup chopped pitted calamite olives 2 tablespoons chopped fresh dill

Directions:

1. Pour the water in a pot over medium heat and bring to a boil. Add the snap peas and 3 teaspoon sea salt (if desired) to the pot and cook for 2 minutes, or until tender crisp. Drain the snap peas and transfer to a bowl. Let rest for 15 minutes to cool completely.
2. Pour the water in the pot over medium heat. Add the faro to the pot and bring to a boil. Cover and cook for 15 to 30 minutes, or until tender. Drain the faro and spread evenly on a baking pan. Let rest for 15 minutes to cool completely.

3. In a large bowl, stir together the olive oil (if desired), lemon juice, shallot, Dijon mustard ¼ teaspoon sea salt (if desired) and ¼ teaspoon black pepper. Add the cooled snap peas, cooled faro, cannellini beans, tomatoes, olives, and dill to the bowl. Toss until well blended. Sprinkle with sea salt (if desired) and pepper to taste.
4. Transfer the salad to 4 to 6 bowls and serve immediately.

Nutrition:

Calories: 501

Fat: 14.9g

Carbs: 81.6g

Protein: 16.6g

Fiber: 7.3g

Wheat Berry Salad with Chickpeas

Preparation time: 25 minutes

Cooking time: 60 minutes

Servings: 4

Ingredients:

- 1½ cups wheat berries
- 16 cups water
- 2 teaspoons sea salt (optional)
- ¼ teaspoon ground black pepper
- 4 teaspoons sherry vinegar
- 2 teaspoons Dijon mustard
- 1 garlic clove, minced
- ¾ teaspoon smoked paprika
- 3 tablespoons extra-virgin olive oil (optional)
- 1 (15-ounce / 425-g) can chickpeas, rinsed
- 3 ounces (85 g) baby spinach, chopped
- 1 small red onion, thinly sliced
- 3 oranges, peeled, pitted and thinly sliced
- ¼ cup minced fresh mint

Directions:

1. Pour the water in a pot over medium heat and bring to a boil. Add the wheat berries and 1½ teaspoons salt (if desired) to the pot and bring to a boil. Reduce the heat to low and simmer for 1 hour to 1 hour 10 minutes, or until the wheat berries become just tender and still chewy. Drain the wheat berries and place on a baking pan to let rest for 15 minutes until completely cool.

2. In a large bowl, stir together the sherry vinegar, Dijon mustard, garlic, smoked paprika, ½ teaspoon salt (if desired), ¼ teaspoon pepper and the olive oil (if desired).

3. Combine the cooled wheat berries, chickpeas, spinach, onion, oranges and mint to the bowl. Toss to blend well.

4. Transfer to bowls and serve immediately.

Nutrition:

Calories: 327

 Fat: 9.3g

 Carbs: 54.7g

 Protein: 10.7g

 Fiber: 4.9g

Chickpea and Heart of Palm Salad

Preparation time: 10 minutes

Cooking time: 0 minutes

Servings: 4

Ingredients:

- 1 (15.5-ounce / 439-g) can chickpeas, drained and rinsed
- 1 (14-ounce / 397-g) can hearts of palm, drained and chopped
- ½ cup diced celery
- ½ cup chopped white onion
- ¼ cup almond butter

- ½ teaspoon sea salt (optional)
- ¼ teaspoon freshly ground black pepper

Directions:

1. Place the chickpeas in a large bowl and mash them into a chunky paste with a hand masher.

2. Make the salad: Add the remaining ingredients to the bowl and toss to combine well.

3. Divide the salad among 4 bowls and serve immediately.

Nutrition:

Calories: 212

Fat: 5.7g

Carbs: 34.8g

Protein: 8.8g

Fiber: 8.1g

Citrus Fruit Salad

Preparation Time: 15 minutes

Servings: 2

Ingredients: For Salad:

- 3 cups fresh kale, tough ribs removed and torn
- 1 orange, peeled and segmented
- 1 grapefruit, peeled and segmented
- 2 tablespoons unsweetened dried cranberries

For Dressing:

- 2 tablespoons extra-virgin olive oil
- 2 tablespoons fresh orange juice
- 1 teaspoon Dijon mustard
- ½ teaspoon raw honey
- Salt and ground black pepper, as required

Directions:

1. For salad: in a salad bowl, place all ingredients and mix.

2. For dressing: place all ingredients in another bowl and beat until well combined.
3. Place dressing on top of salad and toss to coat well.
4. Serve immediately.

Nutrition:

Calories 256

Total Fat 14.5g

Saturated Fat 2.1 g

Cholesterol 0 mg

Sodium 150 mg

Total Carbs 31.3 g

Fiber 4.8 g

Sugar 16.6 g

Protein 4.6 g

Soup

Shrimp & arugula soup

Preparation time: 8 minutes

Cooking time: 32 minutes

Serving: 2

Ingredients:

- 5 large prawns, cleaned deveined and chopped into bite-sized pieces
- 1 red onion, sliced very thinly
- 1 cup arugula
- 1 cup baby kale
- 2 large celery stalks, sliced very thinly
- 5 sprigs of parsley, chopped
- 5 cloves of garlic, minced
- 5 cups of chicken or fish or vegetable stock
- 1 tbsp extra virgin olive oil
- Dash of sea salt
- Dash of black pepper

Directions:

1. Sauté the vegetables (not the kale or arugula), in a stock pot, on low heat for about 2 minutes so that they are still tender and still crunchy, but not cooked quite yet
2. Add the salt and pepper.
3. Add the shrimp to the pot, and sauté for 10 more minutes on medium-low heat (Make sure the shrimp is cooked thoroughly and is not translucent).
4. When the shrimp seems to be cooked through, add the stock to the pot and cook on medium for about 20 more minutes.
5. Remove from heat and cool before serving.

Nutrition:

Calories - 450

Fat - 27g

Carbs – 32g

Protein – 23g

Curry Lentil Soup

Preparation time: 5 minutes

Cooking time: 40 minutes

Servings: 6

Ingredients:

- 1 cup brown lentils
- 1 medium white onion, peeled, chopped
- 28 ounces diced tomatoes
- 1 ½ teaspoon minced garlic
- 1 inch of ginger, grated
- 3 cups vegetable broth
- 1/2 teaspoon salt
- 2 tablespoons curry powder
- 1 teaspoon cumin
- 1/2 teaspoon cayenne
- 1 tablespoon olive oil
- 1 1/2 cups coconut milk, unsweetened
- ¼ cup chopped cilantro

Directions:

1. Take a soup pot, place it over medium-high heat, add oil and when hot, add onion, stir in garlic and ginger and cook for 5 minutes until golden brown.
2. Then add all the ingredients except for milk and cilantro, stir until mixed and simmer for 25 minutes until lentils have cooked.
3. When done, stir in milk, cook for 5 minutes until thoroughly heated and then garnish the soup with cilantro.
4. Serve straight away

Nutrition:

Calories: 269 Cal

Fat: 15 g

Carbs: 26 g

Protein: 10 g

Fiber: 10 g

Chickpea Noodle Soup

Preparation time: 5 minutes

Cooking time: 18 minutes

Servings: 6

Ingredients:

- 1 cup cooked chickpeas
- 8 ounces rotini noodles, whole-wheat
- 4 celery stalks, sliced
- 2 medium white onions, peeled, chopped
- 4 medium carrots, peeled, sliced
- 2 teaspoons minced garlic
- 8 sprigs of thyme
- 1 teaspoon salt
- 1/3 teaspoon ground black pepper
- 1 bay leaf
- 2 tablespoons olive oil
- 2 quarts of vegetable broth
- ¼ cup chopped fresh parsley

Directions:

1. Take a large pot, place it over medium heat, add oil and when hot, add all the vegetables, stir in garlic, thyme and bay leaf and cook for 5 minutes until vegetables are golden and sauté.
2. Then pour in broth stir and bring the mixture to boil.
3. Add chickpeas and noodles into boiling soup, continue cooking for 8 minutes until noodles are tender, and then season soup with salt and black pepper.
4. Garnish with parsley and serve straight away

Nutrition:

Calories: 260 Cal

Fat: 5 g

Carbs: 44 g

Protein: 7 g

Fiber: 4 g

Mexican Lentil Soup

Preparation time: 5 minutes

Cooking time: 45 minutes

Servings: 6

Ingredients:

- 2 cups green lentils
- 1 medium red bell pepper, cored, diced
- 1 medium white onion, peeled, diced
- 2 cups diced tomatoes
- 8 ounces diced green chilies
- 2 celery stalks, diced
- 2 medium carrots, peeled, diced
- 1 ½ teaspoon minced garlic
- 1/2 teaspoon salt
- 1 tablespoon cumin
- 1/4 teaspoon smoked paprika
- 1 teaspoon oregano
- 1/8 teaspoon hot sauce
- 2 tablespoons olive oil

- 8 cups vegetable broth
- ¼ cup cilantro, for garnish
- 1 avocado, peeled, pitted, diced, for garnish

Directions:

1. Take a large pot over medium heat, add oil and when hot, add all the vegetables, reserving tomatoes and chilies, and cook for 5 minutes until softened.
2. Then add garlic, stir in oregano, cumin, and paprika, and continue cooking for 1 minute.
3. Add lentils, tomatoes and green chilies, season with salt, pour in the broth and simmer the soup for 40 minutes until cooked.
4. When done, ladle soup into bowls, top with avocado and cilantro and serve straight away

Nutrition:

Calories: 235 Cal

Fat: 9 g

Carbs: 32 g

Protein: 9 g

Cauliflower Soup

Preparation time: 10 minutes

Cooking time: 40 minutes

Servings: 2

Ingredients: *3 Leeks or a bunch of green onion*

- 1 small head of cauliflower, cut into florets
- 4 tablespoons pomegranate seeds *opt*
- 2 sprigs of thyme and more for garnishing
- 1 teaspoon minced garlic *1 TBLS*
- 2/3 teaspoon salt
- 1/3 teaspoon ground black pepper
- 1 tablespoon olive oil
- 1 1/2 cups vegetable stock

1/2 red onion cubes w/ garlic foil

- 1/2 cup coconut milk, unsweetened *ALMOND*

Directions:

1. Take a pot, place it over medium heat, add oil and when hot, add garlic and cook for 1 minute until fragrant.
2. Add florets, thyme, pour in the stock and bring the mixture to boil.
3. Switch heat to the medium low level, simmer the soup for 30 minutes until florets are tender, then remove the pot from heat, discard the thyme and puree using an immersion blender until smooth.
4. Stir milk into the soup, season with salt and black pepper, then garnish with pomegranate seeds and thyme sprigs and serve.

Nutrition:

Calories: 184 Cal

Fat: 11 g

Carbs: 17 g

Protein: 3 g

Vegan

Spinach and Kale Stir Fry

Preparation Time: 15 Minutes

Cooking Time: 15 Minutes

Servings: 4

Ingredients:

- 2 chopped shallots
- 1 cup no-salt-added and chopped canned tomatoes
- 2 cup baby spinach
- 2 minced garlic cloves
- 5 cup torn kale
- 1 tbsp. extra virgin olive oil

Directions:

1. Heat up a pan with the oil over medium-high heat
2. Add the shallots, stir and sauté for 5 minutes.
3. Add the spinach, kale, and the other ingredients, toss, cook for 10 minutes more.
4. Divide between plates and serve.

Nutrition:

Calories: 141 Cal

Fat: 28 g

Aromatic Red Endives

Preparation Time: 30 Minutes

Cooking Time: 30 Minutes

Servings: 4

Ingredients:

- 2 tbsp. extra virgin olive oil
- 1 tsp. dried rosemary
- 2 halved endives
- ¼ tsp. black pepper
- ½ tsp. turmeric powder

Directions:

1. In a baking pan, combine the endives with the oil and the other ingredients, toss gently.
2. Insert in the oven and bake at 400 0F for 20 minutes.
3. Divide between plates and serve.

Nutrition:

Calories: 102 Cal

Fat: 38 g

Kale & Chicken Stew

Preparation time: 5 Minutes

Cooking Time: 55 Minutes

Servings 4

Ingredients:

- 1 cup sliced leeks
- 1 sliced carrot
- 1 cup chopped onions
- Salt & 1 Tsp. ground pepper to taste
- 2 cups chicken broth
- 3 cups kale
- 4 pounds chicken

Directions:

1. Put ingredients in the slow cooker. Cover, & cook on low for 7 to 9 hours.

Nutrition:

Calories 273

Fat 15

Fiber 11.6

Carbs 16.9

Protein 18.8

Lemony Wax Beans

Preparation time: 5 minutes

Cooking time: 12 minutes

Servings: 4

Ingredients:

- 2 pounds (907 g) wax beans
- 2 tablespoons extra-virgin olive oil
- Salt
- ground black pepper
- Juice of ½ lemon, for serving

Directions:

2. Line a baking sheet with aluminum foil.
3. Toss the wax beans with the olive oil in a large bowl. Lightly season with salt and pepper.
4. Spread out the wax beans on the sheet pan.
5. Select Roast, set temperature to 400°F (205°C), and set time to 12 minutes.
6. Once preheated, place the baking sheet into the oven.

7. When done, the beans will be caramelized and tender. Serve sprinkled with the lemon juice.

Nutrition:

Calories: 44

Carbs: 6g

Fat: 0g

Protein: 2g

Maple and Pecan Granola

Preparation time: 5 minutes

Cooking time: 20 minutes

Servings: 4

Ingredients:

- 1½ cups rolled oats
- ¼ cup maple syrup
- ¼ cup pecan pieces
- 1 teaspoon vanilla extract
- ½ teaspoon ground cinnamon

Directions:

1. Line a baking sheet with parchment paper.
2. Mix the oats, maple syrup, pecan pieces, vanilla, and cinnamon in a large bowl and stir until the oats and pecan pieces are completely coated. Spread the batter on the baking sheet.
3. Set temperature to 300ºF (150ºC), and set time to 20 minutes.
4. Once preheated, place the baking sheet into the oven. Stir once halfway through the cooking time.
5. When done, cool it for 30 minutes before serving. The granola may still be a bit soft right after removing, but it will gradually firm up as it cools.

Nutrition:

Calories: 137

Carbs: 18g

Fat: 6g

Protein: 3g

Sweet and Spicy Broccoli

Preparation time: 10 minutes

Cooking time: 20 minutes

Servings: 4

Ingredients:

- ½ teaspoon olive oil,
- 1 pound (454 g) f broccoli, cut into florets
- ½ tablespoon garlic
- Salt, to taste
- Sauce:
- 1½ tablespoons soy sauce
- 2 teaspoons hot sauce or sriracha
- 1½ teaspoons honey
- 1 teaspoon white vinegar
- Freshly ground black pepper, to taste

Directions:

1. Grease a perforated pan with olive oil.
2. Add the broccoli florets, ½ teaspoon of olive oil, and garlic to a large bowl and toss well—season with salt to taste.
3. Put the broccoli in the perforated pan in a single layer.
4. Select Air Fry, set temperature to 400ºF (205ºC), and set time to 15 minutes.
5. Once preheated, place the pan into the oven. Stir the broccoli florets three times during cooking.
6. Meanwhile, whisk all the ingredients for the sauce in a small bowl until well incorporated.
7. The broccoli should be lightly browned and crispy. Continue cooking for 5 minutes, if desired. Transfer and pour over the sauce and toss to combine. Add more salt and pepper if needed. Serve warm.

Nutrition:

Calories: 68

Carbs: 4g

Fat: 4g

Protein: 3g

Beverages

Chocolate strawberry milk

Preparation time: 5 minutes

Cooking time: 0 minutes

Serving: 1

Ingredients:

- 200 ml milk or dairy-free alternative 150 g strawberries, peeled and halved
- 1 tbsp cocoa powder (100 percent cocoa)
- 10 g pitted Medjool dates
- 10 g walnuts

1 tsp Matcha

Directions:

1. Put all ingredients in a powerful mixer and stir until smooth.
2. Once the matcha has dissolved, add the rest of the juice.

Nutrition:

Carbohydrates: 16

Fat: 6

Protein: 3

Kcal: 130

Green tea and Rocket smoothie

Preparation time: 5 minutes

Cooking time: -0 minutes

Serving: 1

Ingredients:

- 200 ml of water
- 50 g banana, sliced
- 25 g pitted Medjool dates

- 15 g rocket
- 1 teaspoon matcha
- 5 g parsley

Directions:

1. Put all ingredients in a powerful mixer and stir until smooth.
2. Once the matcha has dissolved, add the rest of the juice

Nutrition:

Carbohydrates: 8

Fat: 3

Protein: 1

Kcal: 100

Chocolate strawberry milk

Preparation time: 5 minutes

Cooking time: 0 minutes

Serving: 1

Ingredients:

- 150 g strawberries, peeled and halved
- 1 tbsp cocoa powder (100 percent cocoa)
- 10 g pitted Medjool dates
- 10 g walnuts
- 200 ml milk or dairy-free alternative

1 tsp matcha

Directions:

1. Put all ingredients in a powerful mixer and stir until smooth.
2. Once the matcha has dissolved, add the rest of the juice.

Nutrition:

Carbohydrates: 16

Fat: 6

Protein: 3

Kcal: 130

Pineapple Lassi

Preparation time: 5 minutes

Cooking time: 0 minutes

Serving: 1

Ingredients:

- 200 g pineapple, cut into pieces
- 150 g Greek yogurt   *1 tsp matcha*
- 4–5 ice cubes
- 1 teaspoon ground turmeric

Directions:

1. Put all ingredients in a powerful mixer and stir until smooth.
2. Once the matcha has dissolved, add the rest of the juice. If the mixture is too thick, just add some water and mix until you get the consistency you want.

Nutrition:

Carbohydrates: 13

Fat: 3

Protein: 2

Kcal: 90

Snacks and Desserts

Triple Chocolate Chip Deep Dish Cookies

Preparation Time: 10 minutes

Cooking Time: 30 minutes

Servings: 1

Ingredients:

- 3/4 cup canned pumpkin
- 3/4 cup chocolate peanut butter
- 1/2 cup powdered chocolate protein
- 1/4 cup honey
- 1 beaten egg
- 1 teaspoon pure vanilla
- 1/2 teaspoon baking soda

- 1/2 cup sugar-free chocolate chips
- Vanilla ice cream or serving

Directions:

1. Add all the ingredients except ice cream and chocolate chips in a bowl
2. Use a mixer (electric) beat until mixed evenly.
3. Heat your oven to 350 degrees Fahrenheit.
4. Gradually add the chocolate chips and gently fold to incorporate.
5. Pour batter into a skillet (medium).
6. Place skillet into a preheated oven to bake for approximately 20 minutes until golden brown.
7. Remove from heat and set aside for roughly 7–10 minutes.
8. Serve using the vanilla ice cream.

Nutrition:

Calories: 502

Protein: 6g

Carbohydrates: 65g

Fats: 24g

Protein Brownies

Preparation Time: 10 minutes

Cooking Time: 30–35 minutes

Servings: 1

Ingredients:

- 1/2 cup almond milk
- 1/2 cup, chocolate flavored egg whites
- 1/2 cup, unsweetened apple sauce
- 1/2 cup+1 tablespoon Greek yogurt
- 1 cup, oat flour
- 2–3 scoops, powdered chocolate protein
- 3 tablespoons, powdered unsweetened cocoa
- 1 teaspoon, baker style baking powder
- 1/2 teaspoon salt

Ingredients for the frosting:

- 1/2 cup, nonfat Greek yogurt
- 1/4 cup cherries
- Sweetener (optional)

Directions:

1. The first step is to heat an oven to 350 degrees Fahrenheit then lightly spray a baking dish using cooking spray.
2. Add the egg whites and whisk well until beaten lightly.
3. Add the protein powder, oat flour, sweetener, powdered cocoa, and the baking powder separately.
4. Stir well until mixed evenly, then pour milk mixture (almond) into the flour mixture.
5. Stir well until thoroughly mixed and set batter aside for approximately 5 minutes.
6. Pour batter into the dish and place into the oven to bake for approximately 25 minutes until thoroughly cooked.
7. Remove brownie from heat then set aside to cool.
8. Add all the frosting ingredients in a food processor then process on the highest setting until it becomes smooth.
9. Spread frosting over the top of brownies. Serve.

Nutrition:

Calories: 466

Protein: 6g

Carbohydrates: 50g

Fats: 29g

Protein Pumpkin Spiced Donuts

Preparation Time: 10 minutes

Cooking Time: 15 minutes

Servings: 1

Ingredients:

- 1 cup oat flour
- 3/4 cup xylitol
- 1 scoop, powdered vanilla protein
- 1 tablespoon, ground flaxseed
- 1 tablespoon, ground cinnamon
- 2 teaspoon baking powder
- 1 teaspoon sea salt
- 3 beaten eggs
- 1/2 cup canned pumpkin
- 1 tablespoon melted coconut oil
- 2 teaspoon pure vanilla
- 1 teaspoon apple cider vinegar

Ingredients for the frosting:

- 1/2 cup whipped cream cheese
- 1/2 teaspoon liquid stevia

Directions:

1. Place the xylitol, oat flour, ground flaxseed, powdered protein, baking powder, ground cinnamon, and a dash of sea salt in a large bowl. Preheat your oven to 350°F.
2. Add the egg (beaten) into another bowl (large) along with the pumpkin (canned), pure vanilla, and vinegar and coconut oil (melted).
3. Whisk until mixed (evenly), then pour the mixture into the flour. Stir until thoroughly mixed.
4. Use cooking spray grease a large donut pan.
5. Pour batter into the donut pan (greased).
6. Place batter into the oven and bake for approximately 10 minutes until thoroughly baked.
7. Remove from heat and set donuts onto a wire rack to cool.
8. Add in the cream cheese (whipped) and liquid stevia in a small bowl, whisk until it becomes smooth.
9. Frost donuts using the frosting and serve with a sprinkle of cinnamon (ground) over the top.

Nutrition:

Calories: 452

Protein: 4.9g

Carbohydrates: 51g

Fats: 25g

Wrapped Plums

Preparation Time: 5 Minutes

Cooking Time: 5 Minutes

Servings: 5

Ingredients:

- 2 ounces prosciutto, cut into 16 pieces
- 4 plums, quartered
- 1 tablespoon chives, chopped
- A pinch of red pepper flakes, crushed

Directions:

1. Wrap each plum quarter in a prosciutto slice, arrange them all on a platter, sprinkle the chives and pepper flakes all over and serve.

Nutrition:

Calories 30

Fat 1 g

Fiber 0 g

Carbs 4 g

Protein 2 g

Cucumber Sandwich Bites

Preparation Time: 5 Minutes

Cooking Time: 0 Minutes

Servings: 5

Ingredients:

- 1 cucumber, sliced
- 8 slices whole wheat bread
- 2 tablespoons cream cheese, soft
- 1 tablespoon chives, chopped

- ¼ cup avocado, peeled, pitted and mashed
- 1 teaspoon mustard
- Salt and black pepper to the taste

Directions:

2. Spread the mashed avocado on each bread slice, also spread the rest of the ingredients except the cucumber slices.
3. Divide the cucumber slices on the bread slices, cut each slice in thirds, arrange on a platter and serve as an appetizer.

Nutrition:

Calories 187

Fat 12.4 g

Fiber 2.1 g

Carbs 4.5 g

Protein 8.2 g

Cocoa and Nuts Bombs

Preparation Time: 13 minutes

Cooking time: 8 minutes

Servings: 12

Ingredients:

- 2 cups macadamia nuts; chopped.
- ¼ cup cocoa powder
- 1/3 cup swerve
- 4 tbsp. coconut oil; melted
- 1 tsp. vanilla extract

Directions:

Take a bowl and mix all the ingredients and whisk well.

Shape medium balls out of this mix, place them in your air fryer and cook at 300°F for 8 minutes. Serve cold

Nutrition:

Calories: 120

Fat: 12g

Fiber: 1g

Carbs: 2g

Protein: 1g

Sweet Cinnamon Peaches

Preparation time: 5 minutes

Cooking time: 10 minutes

Servings: 4

Ingredients:

- 2 tablespoons sugar
- ¼ teaspoon ground cinnamon
- 4 peaches, cut into wedges
- Cooking spray

Directions:

1. Grease your air fryer basket using a cooking spray.
2. In a large bowl, stir the sugar and cinnamon. Add the peaches to the bowl and toss to coat evenly.
3. Spread the coated peaches in a single layer on the basket.
4. Select Air Fry, set the temperature to 350°F (180°C), and set time to 10 minutes.
5. After 5 minutes, remove and flip the peaches over. Lightly mist them with cooking spray. Return until done.
6. Let rest for 5 minutes before serving.

Nutrition:

Calories: 80

Carbs: 20g

Fat: 0g

Protein: 0g

Chapter 7: Phase 2 of Sirt-food Diet: Maintenance

In phase 2 of the sirtfood diet, it is expected that you would progress with your fat loss. As phase 2 progresses, if you stick religiously with your diet, you are likely to find yourself getting slimmer and feeling even more energized and pumped to tackle your daily tasks. In phase 2 of the sirtfood diet, you would be eating three times a day, meaning that issues of hunger, fatigue, and irritability due to re-striction of calories should not be a problem here. Even though it is advised that you eat thrice, it is still recommended that you do not over-eat. Eat till you feel reasonably full and satisfied, and then stop. Satisfaction and sustainability are the hallmarks of phase 2, and this phase, if handled well, will help you integrate the sirtfood diet into your lifestyle.

How to Prepare for Phase 2

To help you coast through the second phase of the sirtfood diet successfully, there are trifling pointers that you harmonize and probably start implementing right from your first phase. These tips include:

To ensure that you maximize the benefits of this power drink, it is important that you drink it thirty minutes to one hour before having your main breakfast. Waking up early will help you ensure that you drink your sirtfood green juice, get a little workout done, and get ready for work before finally eating your healthy sirtfood breakfast. The combination of the sirtfood meal and the sirtfood green juice will help fill you up and get you energized to maximize your day, while of course, helping you to melt away those fat deposits along the way.

Eat dinner early: Whether you are on a diet or not, medical experts generally advise against late-might eating. It is healthier to eat your dinner early, between 6 PM and 7 PM, and then get a little rest before retiring to bed. So, instead of working late and wolfing down a heavy dinner in bed at 11 PM, try to take a break, eat your healthy dinner, and then get back to handling the rest of your work. It helps if you are done with your work at least one hour before bed so that you can give your body the opportunity to gradually calm down before you sleep. To ensure the optimal success of the sirtfood diet, you should get an average of 7 -8 hours of sleep per night. If you are extremely busy, try to get at least 6 hours of sleep every night. That will help the nutrients in the food repair and rejuvenate your body cells, which will make you healthier, stronger, and well-built. Sleeping early also generally makes you focused and energized when you wake up to tackle the challenges of the next day.

Eat balanced, measured potions: It is important to strike a balance in the quantity of food you would be eating. Eat too much, and you would be overloading your body with calories. You may think: "But the aim is to get as much of the important chemicals as possible!". Yes, you want to have as many polyphenols as healthily possible into your system, but over-eating can cause constipation and affect the action of the sirtuins in your body. So, eat till you are satiated, and then stop. Since you will be eating three meals per day in the second phase, there is no need for you to overload yourself at any time. Eat till you feel reasonably satisfied, get to work, and then eat another meal later. You don't have to go hungry, but you don't have to overload yourself to the point of lethargy either. Let your appetite guide you and stay energized and focused.

Drink your sirtfood juice once: The sirtfood juice is an excellent source of nutrients and polyphenols for activating your sirtuin genes. However, as you progress with the diet and eat more food on a daily basis, you are required to gradually begin to slow down your consumption of the sirtfood green juice., You will recall that in Phase 1, the sirtfood green juice was recommended to be consumed thrice per day alongside one mail for the first three days. In the last four days of phase 1, the recommended daily intake of the sirtfood green juice reduces to two cups, and you become required to eat two meals per day. Once you transition into phase 2 of your diet, however, things change. You can now eat three meals per day, meaning you can get an optimum supply of your nutrients from your food, and intense calorie restriction is no longer necessary. For this reason, once phase 2 begins, you should only consume your sirtfood green juice only once a day – and that's very early in the morning, thirty minutes to one hour before your main breakfast.

Apart from the sirtfood green juice, you can still drink a couple of liquids in phase 2 of the diet. These liquids include water, flavored water, black coffee, and green tea. You may also consume red wine up to three times a week as soon as you commence phase 2.

Expectations for Phase 2

In phase 2, your weight loss journey will continue. The amount of fat that would be eradicated in this phase would vary from one individual to another. However, it is not unconventional for people to lose up to 10 more pounds in pure fat in this phase. As we constantly advise, do not try to judge the success of your dieting efforts by checking a weighing scale every morning. The diet is aimed to help you burn fat and improve your muscle mass, so while losing fat, your muscle cells may be actively dividing, thereby helping you to increase your muscle mass. To help you track your fat loss rate, you can look at your body periodically in the mirror, check the fit of your clothes, or ask for a few trusted opinions.

Phase 2 will also come with enhanced focus and vitality. The active components of the sirtfoods will continue to keep your sirtuin genes activated, leading to feelings of enhanced mental clarity and boosted concentration. The consumption of the foods contained in the sirtfood diet helps to rejuvenate your brain cells, thereby helping to improve brainpower.

If you were addicted to junk food and sugary products prior to staring the sirtfood diet, phase 2 is the stage where your cravings begin to lessen considerably. This is because you would be having three healthy meals per day, and a nutrient-packed cup of green juice to start your day with. Your body would constantly feel satiated, and that urge to dash across the street to grab a burger and a soda just won't be there since you would not be feeling hungry in the first place.

In the long-term, completing phase 2 of the sirtfood diet and moving on to integrate the sirtfood diet system into your lifestyle would help reduce your susceptibility to debilitating diseases. The consumption of unhealthy food leads to the accumulation of fat deposits in the body, as has been described earlier in this book. When you consume a lot of sugar processed regularly, the sugar will gain easy access to your bloodstream, increasing your blood sugar levels, and by extension, your insulin levels. Once your insulin levels pass a certain safe threshold, the natural burning of fats in the body is suppressed, and you begin to trend towards obesity. With obesity comes a high likelihood of heart disease since the fats would make it compulsory for the heart to pump blood at unhealthily high pressure. In some cases, the fat deposits may even block key blood vessels within the body, which can lead to falling unconscious and even death.

Meal Plan for Phase 2

Throughout the fourteen days of phase 2, you will be drinking one serving of sirtfood juice very early in the morning at least thirty minutes to one hour before food. You will also be consuming three standard meals a day – breakfast, lunch, and dinner. These meals will provide your body with the necessary calories and nutrients it needs to stay energized and satiated while eradicating unhealthy fat deposits and repairing your body's cells. In phase 2, carefully selected sirtfood snacks may also be introduced, and they may be consumed once or twice per day. The sirtfood snacks can particularly come in handy when you are in a position where you cannot have a standard meal right away. So instead of violating your diet's rules and eating unhealthy junk, you can simply have a healthy sirtfood snack, pending the time you can eat a standard meal. Sirtfood snacks can be particularly great for long meetings, flights, and long road travels, shopping, and other related circumstances.

Also, one final reminder, the sirtfood diet works best when the foods digest and get the chance to start working before you go to bed, so your dinner should not exceed 7 PM.

Breakfast Options

The foods in this section may be eaten at 7-day intervals. Depending on your preferences and your schedule, however, you can modify this suggestion to fit your lifestyle. Meal option one may be eaten on the eighth day of your diet and the 15th day, for instance. Meal 2 may be eaten on day 9 of the diet and day 16. The point is to make the food as varied as possible and to eat as many meals as possible before consuming the same food again.

The breakfast options include:

Sirtfood smoothie

Sirt muesli

Yogurt, berries, walnut and dark chocolate

Spicy scrambled eggs

Mushroom/ tofu scramble

Buckwheat pancakes, walnuts, strawberries and chocolate

Sirtfood omelet.

Lunch options

Just as instructed for the breakfast options, the lunch options may also be eaten once a week, preferably on a specific day of the week to help you vary your diet and find your new feeding regimen interesting.

Lunch options include:

Sirt chicken salad.

Waldorf salad – apples, walnuts, celery, and mayonnaise.

Sirt tuna salad.

Strawberry buckwheat salad.

Buckwheat pasta salad.

Tofu and shiitake mushroom soup

Whole wheat leavened bread.

Dinner options

Foods that may be eaten for dinner during phase 2 of the sirtfood diet include:

Stir-fry shrimp and buckwheat noodles.

Tuscan bean stew.

Potatoes, kale, curry, and chicken.

Kale, red onions and buckwheat

Sirt chili con carne

Kidney bean mole and baked potatoes

Sirtfood pizza.

Breakfast Recipes

Buckwheat Granola

Preparation Time: 15 minutes

Cooking Time: 30 minutes

Servings: 10

Ingredients:

- 2 cups raw buckwheat groats
- ¾ cup pumpkin seeds
- ¾ cup almonds, chopped
- 1 cup unsweetened coconut flakes
- 1 teaspoon ground cinnamon
- 1 teaspoon ground ginger
- 1 ripe banana, peeled
- 2 tablespoons maple syrup
- 2 tablespoons olive oil

Directions:

1. Preheat your oven to 350 °F.
2. In a bowl, place the buckwheat groats, coconut flakes pumpkin seeds, almonds and spices and mix well.
3. In another bowl, add the banana and with a fork, mash well.
4. Add to the buckwheat mixture, maple syrup and oil and mix until well combined.
5. Transfer the mixture onto the prepared baking sheet and spread in an even layer.
6. Bake for approximately 25-30 minutes, stirring once halfway through.
7. Remove the baking sheet from oven and set aside to cool.

Nutrition:

Calories 252

Total Fat 14.3 g

Saturated Fat 3.7 g

Cholesterol 0 mg

Sodium 5 mg

Total Carbs 27.6 g

Fiber 4.9 g

Sugar 4.9 g

Protein 7.6 g

Sirtfood Muffins

Preparation Time: 25 minutes

Cooking Time: 2 hours 16 minutes

Servings: 18

Ingredients:

- 1 cup milk
- 2 tbsps. White sugar
- 1 (.25 oz.) package active dry yeast
- 1 cup warm water (110 degrees F/45 degrees C)
- 1/4 cup melted shortening
- 6 cups all-purpose flour
- 1 tsp. salt

Directions:

1. In a small saucepan, warm milk until it is bubbling. Take away from the heat. Add sugar while stirring until it is dissolved. Allow cooling to lukewarm. Dissolve the yeast in warm water in a small bowl and leave to sit for about 10 minutes until creamy.
2. Combine 3 cups flour, shortening, yeast mixture, and milk in a large bowl. Then beat until the mix is smooth. Pour in salt and remaining flour or enough of it to form a soft dough. Knead and transfer into a greased bowl. Cover the dough and leave it to rise.
3. Press down and then roll out into about half inch thick. Use empty tuna can, drinking glass or a biscuit cutter to cut the rounds. Drizzle cornmeal onto waxed paper and leave the rounds to rise on this. Dust cornmeal onto the tops of muffins. Cover them and allow rising for 1/2 hour.
4. Heat griddle that is greased and then cook the muffins for about 10 minutes per side in the griddle over medium heat. Keep the baked muffins in a warm oven until all are cooked. Cool, transfer into plastic bags and store.
5. To use, cut and then toast. Good together with jam, cream cheese or orange butter.

Nutrition:

Calories per serving: 163

Carbohydrates: 45.6 g

Protein: 3 g

Fat: 0.6g

Sugar: 1g

Sodium: 87mg

Fiber: .7 g

Fruity Tofu Smoothie

Preparation Time: 5 Minutes

Cooking Time: 0 Minutes

Servings: 2

Ingredients:

- 1 c. ice cold water
- 1 c. packed spinach
- ¼ c. frozen mango chunks
- ½ c. frozen pineapple chunks
- 1 tbsp. chia seeds
- 1 container silken tofu
- 1 frozen medium banana

Directions:

1. Add all ingredients in a blender until smooth and creamy.
2. Evenly divide into two glasses, serve and enjoy.

Nutrition:

Calories: 175

Fat: 3.7 g

Carbs: 33.3 g

Protein: 6.0 g

Black currants and oat yogurt

Preparation time: 10 minutes

Cooking time: 0 minutes

Serving: 2

Ingredients:

- 100 g black currants, washed and stems removed
- 2 tbsp powdered sugar + 100 ml water
- 200 g natural yogurt
- 40 g jumbo oats

Directions:

1. Put the black currants, sugar and water in a small pan and bring to a boil. Reduce the heat slightly, simmer vigorously, and continue cooking for 5 minutes.
2. Turn off the stove and let it cool down. The blackcurrant compote can now be refrigerated until it is used. Place the yogurt and oats in a large bowl and stir together. Divide the blackcurrant compote between two bowls and top with yogurt and oats. Use a cocktail stick to toss the compote through the yogurt.

Nutrition:

241 calories

Easy Granola Clusters

Preparation time: 5 minutes

Cooking time: 1 minutes

Servings: 2 cups

Ingredients:

- 1½ cups peanut butter
- ¼ cup maple syrup (optional)
- 1½ cups old-fashioned rolled oats
- ½ cup raisins
- ¾ cup flaxseed meal
- ¾ cup raw sunflower seeds (no shells)

Direction:

1. Place the peanut butter and maple syrup (if desired) in a medium microwave-

safe bowl. Microwave them on high for 30-second intervals, stirring between intervals, or until the mixture is well incorporated and smooth. Allow to cool for a few minutes.
2. Fold in the oats, raisins, flaxseed meal, and sunflower seeds and stir the ingredients until they are completely combined.
3. Spread the mixture evenly on a baking sheet and freeze for at least 25 minutes until firm.
4. Break it into clusters before serving.

Nutrition:

Calories: 493

Fat: 31.0g

Carbs: 49.8g

Protein: 16.0g

Fiber: 12.2g

Stovetop Granola

Preparation time: 5 minutes

Cooking time: 10 minutes

Servings: 6 cups

Ingredients:

- 5 cups rolled oats
- ¾ cup date molasses or brown rice syrup (optional)
- 1 tablespoon ground cinnamon
- ½ teaspoon salt (optional)
- 1 cup chopped dried fruit

Directions:

1. Place the oats in a saucepan over medium-low heat and toast for 4 to 5 minutes, stirring constantly to prevent burning, or until the oats are lightly toasted. Transfer the toasted oats to a medium bowl.
2. Add the date molasses (if desired) to the saucepan and cook over medium-low

heat for 1 minute. Stir in the toasted oats, cinnamon, and salt (if desired). Transfer the mixture to a nonstick baking sheet and allow to cool to room temperature.

3. When cooled, transfer the mixture to a large bowl and add the dried fruit and mix well. Serve immediately.

Nutrition:

Calories: 327

Fat: 5.7g

Carbs: 69.2g

Protein: 14.5g

Fiber: 14.9g

No Bake Peanut Butter Granola Bars

Preparation time: 10 minutes

Cooking time: 0 minutes

Servings: 12 bars

Ingredients:

- 1 cup packed pitted dates
- ¼ cup creamy natural peanut butter or almond butter
- ¼ cup pure maple syrup (optional)
- 1½ cups old-fashioned oats
- 1 cup coarsely chopped roasted unsalted almonds

Directions:

1. Pulse the dates, peanut butter, and maple syrup (if desired) in a food processor until the mixture starts to come together and feels slightly sticky. Stop right before or as it starts to turn into a ball of loose dough.
2. Add the oats and almonds and pulse for 1 minute. Transfer the dough to a baking dish and cover with plastic wrap. Place in the refrigerator for 20 minutes until chilled.
3. Cut into 12 bars and serve immediately.

Nutrition:

Calories: 182

Fat: 8.8g

Carbs: 24.3g

Protein: 5.1g

Fiber: 4.2g

Banana Muesli with Dates

Preparation time: 5 minutes

Cooking time: 0 minutes

Servings: 2

Ingredients:

- 1 banana, peeled and sliced
- 1 cup rolled oats
- ½ cup pitted and chopped dates
- ¾ cup unsweetened almond milk
- ¼ cup unsweetened coconut, toasted

Directions:

1. Mix together all the ingredients in a large bowl until well combined and let soak 15 minutes, or until all the milk is absorbed.
2. Give it a good stir and serve immediately.

Nutrition:

Calories: 391

Fat: 8.1g

Carbs: 82.1g

Protein: 10.5g

Fiber: 13.0g

Apple Muesli

Preparation time: 5 minutes

Cooking time: 0 minutes

Servings: 2

Ingredients:

- 1 cup rolled oats

- .½ cup raisins
- ¾ cup unsweetened almond milk
- 2 tablespoons date molasses or brown rice syrup (optional)
- ¼ teaspoon ground cinnamon
- 1 Granny Smith apple, cored and chopped

Directions:

1. Stir together the oats, raisins, almond milk, date molasses (if desired), and cinnamon in a large bowl and let soak 15 minutes.
2. When ready, add the chopped apple and stir to combine. Serve immediately.

Nutrition:

Calories: 356

Fat: 4.7g

Carbs: 79.9g

Protein: 10.1g

Fiber: 11.5g

Blueberry Oatmeal

Preparation time: 5 minutes

Cooking time: 5 minutes

Servings: 2

Ingredients:

- 1½ cups unsweetened coconut milk
- 1 cup old-fashioned rolled oats
- ½ cup fresh or frozen blueberries, thawed if frozen
- Optional Toppings:
- 2 tablespoons chopped nuts
- 2 to 3 tablespoons granola
- 1 tablespoon maple syrup (optional)
- 2 tablespoons raw sunflower seeds (no shells)
- 1 tablespoon coconut shreds
- 1 teaspoon spices of your choice (like cinnamon or pumpkin pie spice)

Directions:

1. Heat the milk in a medium saucepan over medium-high heat until boiling.
2. Fold in the oats and blueberries and stir well.
3. Reduce the heat to low and let simmer uncovered for 5 minutes, or until the water is absorbed, stirring occasionally.
4. Remove from the heat and top with toppings of choice.

Nutrition:

Calories: 273

Fat: 7.5g

Carbs: 45.4g

Protein: 14.4g

Fiber: 8.5g

Vanilla Steel-Cut Oatmeal

Preparation time: 5 minutes

Cooking time: 40 minutes

Servings: 4

Ingredients:

- 4 cups water
- Pinch sea salt (optional)
- 1 cup steel-cut oats
- ¾ cup unsweetened almond milk
- 2 teaspoons pure vanilla extract

Directions:

1. Place the water and salt (if desired) into a large pot over high heat and bring to a boil.
2. Reduce the heat to low and stir in the oats. Cook for about 30 minutes until the oats are soften, stirring occasionally.
3. Add the milk and vanilla and stir well. Cook for about 10 minutes more until your desired consistency is reached.
4. Remove the cereal from the heat and serve warm.

Nutrition:

Calories: 187

Fat: 0g

Carbs: 28.8g

Protein: 9.2g

Fiber: 5.0g

Easy and Healthy Oatmeal

Preparation time: 5 minutes

Cooking time: 5 minutes

Servings: 2

Ingredients:

- 1 cup rolled oats
- Sea salt, to taste (optional)
- 2 cups unsweetened coconut milk or water

Directions:

1. Cook the oats, salt (if desired), and milk in a small saucepan over medium-high heat. Bring to a boil.
2. Reduce the heat to medium and continue to cook for about 5 minutes, or until the oats have soaked up most of the liquid and are creamy, stirring occasionally.
3. Ladle into bowls and serve hot.

Nutrition:

Calories: 300

Fat: 11.2g

Carbs: 42.7g

Protein: 15.8g

Fiber: 7.2g

Slow Cooker Butternut Squash Oatmeal

Preparation time: 15 minutes

Cooking time: 6 hours

Servings: 4

Ingredients:

- 1 cup steel-cut oats
- 3 cups water
- 2 cups cubed (½-inch pieces) peeled butternut squash
- ¼ cup unsweetened coconut milk
- 1 tablespoon chia seeds
- 1½ teaspoons ground ginger
- 2 teaspoons yellow (mellow) miso paste
- 1 tablespoon sesame seeds, toasted
- 1 tablespoon chopped scallion, green parts only

Directions:

1. Mix together the oats, water, and butternut squash in a slow cooker.
2. Cover and cook on Low for 6 to 8 hours, or until the squash is tender when tested with a fork. Mash the cooked butternut squash with a potato masher or heavy spoon. Stir together the butternut squash and oats until well mixed.
3. Mix together the milk, chia seeds, ginger, and miso paste in a small bowl and stir to combine. Add this mixture to the squash mixture and stir well.
4. Ladle the oatmeal into bowls and serve hot topped with sesame seeds and scallion.

Nutrition:

Calories: 229

Fat: 4.9g

Carbs: 39.7g

Protein: 7.1g

Fiber: 9.0g

Multigrain Hot Cereal with Apricots

Preparation time: 30 minutes

Cooking time: 30 minutes

Servings: 2

Ingredients:

- ¼ cup long-grain brown rice
- 2 tablespoons rye
- 2 tablespoons millet
- 2 tablespoons wheat berries
- 2 tablespoons barley
- 6 dried apricots, chopped

2 cups water

Directions:

1. Rinse the grains and soak them in water for 30 minutes until softened and drain.
2. In a saucepan, add the soaked grains, apricots, and 2 cups of water and stir to combine.
3. Cook for about 17 minutes over low heat, or until the liquid is absorbed, stirring periodically.
4. Allow to cool for 15 minutes before serving.

Nutrition:

Calories: 242

Fat: 1.6g

Carbs: 50.5g

Protein: 6.5g

Fiber: 6.1g

Hot Breakfast Couscous Cereal

Preparation time: 10 minutes

Cooking time: 6 minutes

Servings: 4

Ingredients:

- ¾ cup water
- ½ cup couscous
- ¼ cup squeezed orange juice
- 1 tablespoon maple syrup (optional)
- 1 tablespoon frozen apple juice
- 1 teaspoon finely grated orange zest
- Dash ground cinnamon

Directions:

1. In a large casserole dish, add all the ingredients and stir well. Cover in aluminum foil.
2. Transfer the dish to a microwave oven and cook for 5 to 6 minutes on high heat, stirring occasionally to prevent sticking.
3. Let sit for another 1 minute, covered.
4. Divide the cereal among bowls and serve hot.

Nutrition:

Calories: 47

Fat: 0.3g

Carbs: 10.3g

Protein: 0.9g

Fiber: 0.5g

Apple Pancakes

Preparation Time: 15 minutes

Cooking Time: 24 minutes

Servings: 6

Ingredients:

- ½ cup buckwheat flour
- 2 tablespoons coconut sugar
- 1 teaspoon baking powder
- ½ teaspoon ground cinnamon
- 1/3 cup unsweetened almond milk
- 1 egg, beaten lightly
- 2 granny smith apples, peeled, cored and grated

Directions:

1. In a bowl, place the flour, coconut sugar and cinnamon and mix well.
2. In another bowl, place the almond milk and egg and beat until well combined.
3. Now, place the flour mixture and mix until well combined.
4. Fold in the grated apples.
5. Heat a lightly greased nonstick wok over medium-high heat.

6. Add desired amount of mixture and with a spoon, spread into an even layer.
7. Cook for 1-2 minutes on each side.
8. Repeat with the remaining mixture.
9. Serve warm with the drizzling of honey.

Nutrition:

Calories 93

Total Fat 2.1 g

Saturated Fat 1 g

Cholesterol 27 mg

Sodium 23 mg

Total Carbs 22 g

Fiber 3 g

Sugar 12.1 g

Protein 2.5 g

Lunch
Asparagus Soup

Preparation time: 5 minutes

Cooking time: 28 minutes

Servings: 6

Ingredients:

- 4 pounds potatoes, peeled, chopped
- 1 bunch of asparagus
- 15 ounces cooked cannellini beans
- 1 small white onion, peeled, diced
- 3 teaspoons minced garlic
- 1 teaspoon grated ginger
- ½ teaspoon salt
- ¼ teaspoon ground black pepper
- 1 lemon, juiced
- 1 tablespoon olive oil
- 8 cups vegetable broth

Directions:

1. Place oil in a large pot, place it over medium heat and let it heat until hot.

2. Add onion into the pot, stir in garlic and ginger and then cook for 5 minutes until onion turns tender.
3. Add potatoes, asparagus, and beans, pour in the broth, stir until mixed, and then bring the mixture to a boil.
4. Cook the potatoes for 20 minutes until tender, remove the pot from heat and then puree half of the soup until smooth.
5. Add salt, black pepper, and lemon juice, stir until mixed, ladle soup into bowls and then serve.

Nutrition:

Calories: 123.3

Fat: 4.4 g

Protein: 4.7 g

Carbs: 16.3 g

Fiber: 4.1 g

Kale White Bean Pork chops

Preparation Time: 5 minutes

Cooking Time: 45 minutes

Servings: 4-6

Ingredients:

- 3 tbsp extra-virgin olive oil
- 3 tbsp chili powder
- 1 tbsp jalapeno hot sauce
- 2 pounds bone-in pork chops
- Salt
- 4 stalks celery, chopped
- 1 large white onion, chopped
- 3 cloves garlic, chopped
- 2 cups chicken broth
- 2 cups diced tomatoes
- 2 cups cooked white beans
- 6 cups packed kale

Directions:

1. Preheat the broiler.

2. Whisk hot sauce, 1 tbsp olive oil and chili powder in a bowl.
3. Season the pork chops with ½ tsp salt.
4. Rub chops with the spice mixture on both sides and place them on a rack set over a baking sheet.
5. Set aside.
6. Heat 1 tbsp olive oil in a pot over medium heat.
7. Add the celery, garlic, onion, and the remaining 2 tbsp chili powder.
8. Cook until onions are translucent, stirring (approx. 8 minutes).

Nutrition:

Calories: 140

Fat: 6 g

Carbohydrates: 14 g

Protein: 7 g

Fiber: 3 g

Tuna Salad

Preparation Time: 5 minutes

Cooking Time: 40 minutes

Servings: 3

Ingredients:

- 100g red chicory
- 150g tuna flakes in brine, drained
- 100g cucumber
- 25g rocket
- 6 kalamata olives, pitted
- 2 hard-boiled eggs, peeled and quartered
- 2 tomatoes, chopped
- 2 tbsp fresh parsley, chopped
- 1 red onion, chopped
- 1 celery stalk
- 1 tbsp capers
- 2 tbsp garlic vinaigrette

Directions:

1. Combine all ingredients in a bowl and serve.

Nutrition:

Calories: 240 Cal

Fat: 15 g

Carbohydrates: 7 g

Protein: 23 g

Fiber: 0 g

Turkey Curry

Preparation Time: 5 minutes

Cooking Time: 40 minutes

Servings: 3

Ingredients:

- 450g (1lb), turkey breasts, chopped
- 100g (3½ oz) fresh rocket (arugula) leaves
- 5 cloves garlic, chopped
- 3 tsp medium curry powder
- 2 tsp turmeric powder
- 2 tbsp fresh coriander (cilantro), finely chopped
- 2 bird's eye chilies, chopped
- 2 red onions, chopped
- 400ml (14fl oz) full-fat coconut milk
- 2 tbsp olive oil

Directions:

2. Heat the olive oil in a saucepan, add the chopped red onions and cook them for around 5 minutes or until soft.
3. Stir in the garlic and the turkey and cook it for 7-8 minutes.
4. Stir in the turmeric, chilies and curry powder then add the coconut milk and coriander cilantro).
5. Bring it to the boil, reduce the heat and simmer for around 10 minutes.
6. Scatter the rocket (arugula) onto plates and spoon the curry on top.
7. Serve alongside brown rice.

Nutrition:

Calories: 400

Fat:6 g

Carbohydrates: 3 g

Protein: 14 g

Fiber: 0 g

Tofu and Curry

Preparation Time: 5 minutes

Cooking Time: 36 minutes

Servings: 4

Ingredients:

- 8 oz dried lentils (red preferably)
- 1 cup boiling water
- 1 cup frozen edamame (soy) beans
- 7 oz (½ of most packages) firm tofu, chopped into cubes
- 2 tomatoes, chopped
- 1 lime juices
- 5-6 kale leaves, stalks removed and torn
- 1 large onion, chopped
- 4 cloves garlic, peeled and grated
- 1 large chunk of ginger, grated
- ½ red chili pepper, deseeded (use less if too much)
- ½ tsp ground turmeric
- ¼ tsp cayenne pepper
- 1 tsp paprika
- ½ tsp ground cumin
- 1 tsp salt
- 1 tbsp olive oil

Directions:

1. Add the onion, sauté in the oil for few minutes then add the chili, garlic, and ginger for a bit longer until wilted but not burned.
2. Add the seasonings, then the lentils and stir

Nutrition:

Calories: 250

Fat: 5 g

Carbohydrates: 15 g

Protein: 28 g

Fiber: 1 g

Chicken and Bean Casserole

Preparation Time: 5 minutes

Cooking Time: 40 minutes

Servings: 3

Ingredients:

- 400g (14oz) chopped tomatoes
- 400g (14oz) tinned cannellini beans or haricot beans
- 8 chicken thighs, skin removed
- 2 carrots, peeled and finely chopped
- 2 red onions, chopped
- 4 sticks of celery
- 4 large mushrooms
- 2 red peppers (bell peppers), deseeded and chopped
- 1 clove of garlic
- 2 tbsp soy sauce
- 1 tbsp olive oil
- 1.75 liters (3 pints) chicken stock (broth)

Directions:

1. Heat the olive oil in a saucepan, put in garlic and onions and cook for 5 minutes.
2. Add in the chicken and cook for 5 minutes then add the carrots, cannellini beans, celery, red peppers (bell peppers) and mushrooms.
3. Pour in the stock (broth) soy sauce and tomatoes.
4. Bring it to the boil, reduce the heat and simmer for 45 minutes.
5. Serve with rice or new potatoes.

Nutrition:

Calories: 324

Fat: 11 g

Carbohydrates: 27 g

Protein: 28 g

Fiber: 7 g

Prawn and Coconut Curry

Preparation Time: 5 minutes

Cooking Time: 35 minutes

Servings: 3

Ingredients:

- 400g (14oz) tinned chopped tomatoes
- 400g (14oz) large prawns (shrimps), shelled and raw
- 25g (1oz) fresh coriander (cilantro) chopped
- 3 red onions, finely chopped
- 3 cloves of garlic, crushed
- 2 bird's eye chilies
- ½ tsp ground coriander (cilantro)
- ½ tsp turmeric
- 400ml (14fl oz) coconut milk
- 1 tbsp olive oil
- Juice of 1 lime

Directions:

1. Place the onions, garlic, tomatoes, chilies, lime juice, turmeric, ground coriander (cilantro), chilies and half of the fresh coriander (cilantro) into a blender and blitz until you have a smooth curry paste.
2. Heat the olive oil in a frying pan, add the paste and cook for 2 minutes.
3. Stir in the coconut milk and warm it thoroughly.
4. Add the prawns (shrimps) to the paste and cook them until they have turned pink and are thoroughly cooked.
5. Stir in the fresh coriander (cilantro).
6. Serve with rice.

Nutrition:

Calories: 163

Fat: 8 g

Carbohydrates: 8 g

Protein: 0 g

Fiber: 1 g

Moroccan Chicken Casserole

Preparation Time: 5 minutes

Cooking Time: 20 minutes

Servings: 3

Ingredients:

- 250g (9oz) tinned chickpeas (garbanzo beans) drained
- 4 chicken breasts, cubed
- 4 Medjool dates halved
- 6 dried apricots, halved
- 1 red onion, sliced
- 1 carrot, chopped
- 1 tsp ground cumin
- 1 tsp ground cinnamon
- 1 tsp ground turmeric
- 1 bird's eye chili, chopped
- 600ml (1 pint) chicken stock (broth)
- 25g (1oz) corn flour
- 60ml (2fl oz) water
- 2 tbsp fresh coriander

Directions:

1. Place the chicken, chickpeas (garbanzo beans), onion, carrot, chili, cumin, turmeric, cinnamon, and stock (broth) into a large saucepan.
2. Bring it to the boil, reduce the heat and simmer for 25 minutes.
3. Add in the dates and apricots and simmer for 10 minutes.
4. In a cup, mix the corn flour with the water until it becomes a smooth paste.
5. Pour the mixture into the saucepan and stir until it thickens.

6. Add in the coriander (cilantro) and mix well.

Nutrition:

Calories: 423

Fat: 12 g

Carbohydrates: 0 g

Protein: 39 g

Fiber: 0 g

Chili con Carne

Preparation Time: 5 minutes

Cooking Time: 30 minutes

Servings: 3

Ingredients:

- 450g (1lb) lean minced beef
- 400g (14oz) chopped tomatoes
- 200g (7oz) red kidney beans
- 2 tbsp tomato purée
- 2 cloves of garlic, crushed
- 2 red onions, chopped
- 2 bird's eye chilies, finely chopped
- 1 red pepper (bell pepper), chopped
- 1 stick of celery, finely chopped
- 1 tbsp cumin
- 1 tbsp turmeric
- 1 tbsp cocoa powder
- 400ml (14 oz) beef stock (broth)
- 175ml (6fl oz) red wine
- 1 tbsp olive oil

Directions:

1. Heat the oil in a large saucepan, add the onion and cook for 5 minutes.
2. Add in the garlic, celery, chili, turmeric, and cumin and cook for 2 minutes before adding then meat then cook for another 5 minutes.
3. Pour in the stock (broth), red wine, tomatoes, tomato purée, red pepper (bell pepper), kidney beans and cocoa powder.

Nutrition:

Calories: 320

Fat: 21 g

Carbohydrates: 8 g

Protein: 24 g

Fiber: 4 g

Tofu Thai Curry

Preparation Time: 5 minutes

Cooking Time: 30 minutes

Servings: 3

Ingredients:

- 400g (14oz) tofu, diced
- 200g (7oz) sugar snap peas
- 5cm (2-inch) chunk fresh ginger root, peeled and finely chopped
- 2 red onions, chopped
- 2 cloves of garlic, crushed
- 2 bird's eye chilies
- 2 tbsp tomato puree
- 1 stalk of lemongrass, inner stalks only
- 1 tbsp fresh coriander (cilantro), chopped
- 1 tsp cumin
- 300ml (½ pint) coconut milk
- 200ml (7fl oz) vegetable stock (broth)
- 1 tbsp virgin olive oil
- juice of 1 lime

Directions:

1. Heat the oil in a frying pan, add the onion and cook for 4 minutes.
2. Add in the chilies, cumin, ginger, and garlic and cook for 2 minutes.
3. Add the tomato puree, lemongrass, sugar-snap peas, lime juice and tofu and cook for 2 minutes.

4. Pour in the stock (broth), coconut milk and coriander (cilantro) and simmer for 5 minutes.
5. Serve with brown rice or buckwheat and a handful of rockets (arugula) leaves on the side.

Nutrition:

Calories: 412

Fat: 30 g

Carbohydrates: 27 g

Protein: 14 g

Fiber: 5 g

Roast Balsamic Vegetables

Ingredients:

- 4 tomatoes, chopped
- 2 red onions, chopped
- 3 sweet potatoes, peeled and chopped
- 100g (3½ oz) red chicory (or if unavailable, use yellow)
- 100g (3½ oz) kale, finely chopped
- 300g (11oz) potatoes, peeled and chopped
- 5 stalks of celery, chopped
- 1 bird's eye chili, deseeded and finely chopped
- 2 tbsp fresh parsley, chopped
- 2 tbsp fresh coriander (cilantro) chopped
- 3 tbsp olive oil
- 2 tbsp balsamic vinegar
- 1 tsp mustard
- Sea salt
- Freshly ground black pepper

Directions:

1. Place the olive oil, balsamic, mustard, parsley, and coriander (cilantro) into a bowl and mix well.

2. Toss all the remaining ingredients into the dressing and season with salt and pepper.
3. Transfer the vegetables to an ovenproof dish and cook in the oven at 200C/400F for 45 minutes.

Nutrition:

Calories: 70

Fat: 0 g

Carbohydrates: 8 g

Protein: 2 g

Fiber: 2 g

Chickpea Salad

Preparation time: 5 minutes

Cooking time: 0 minutes

Servings: 2

Ingredients:

- 1 cup cooked chickpeas
- 16 leaves of butter lettuce
- 1 cup chopped zucchini
- ½ spring onion, chopped
- 1 cup chopped celery
- 1 cup grated carrot
- 1 tablespoon chopped cilantro
- ½ teaspoon salt
- ½ tablespoon lemon juice

Directions:

1. Take a large bowl, place all the ingredients in it, toss until mixed, and let it sit for 15 minutes.
2. Divide the lettuce leaves between two portions, top with the salad evenly and then serve.

Nutrition:

Calories: 166.6

Fat: 7.7 g

Protein: 4.4 g

Carbs: 20.8 g

Fiber: 4.3 g

Tofu and Pesto Sandwich

Preparation time: 5 minutes

Cooking time: 15 minutes

Servings: 4

Ingredients:

- 12 ounces of tofu, pressed, drained
- 4 leaves of butter lettuce
- 4 slices of tomato
- 4 tablespoons basil pesto
- 1 tablespoon olive oil
- 4 slices of whole-wheat sandwich bread

Directions:

1. Switch on the oven, then set it to 375 degrees F and let it preheat.
2. Cut tofu into slices, place them in a bowl, and drizzle with oil and then sprinkle with oregano.
3. Spread tofu pieces on a baking sheet and then roast for 15 minutes.
4. Assemble the sandwich and for this, spread 1 tablespoon of basil pesto on one side of each sandwich slice, top with a lettuce leaf, tomato slice, and tofu.
5. Serve straight away.

Nutrition:

Calories: 219

Fat: 13.5 g

Protein: 8 g

Carbs: 18.5 g

Fiber: 4 g

Dinner

Beef bourguignon with Mashed potatoes and kale

Preparation time: 15 minutes

Cooking time: 2 - 3 hours

Serving: 4

Ingredients:

- 800 g diced beef
- 2–3 tbsp buckwheat flour
- 1 tbsp extra virgin olive oil
- 150 g red onion, roughly chopped
- 200 g celery, roughly chopped
- 100 g carrots, roughly chopped
- 2–3 cloves of garlic, chopped
- 375 ml of red wine
- 2 tbsp tomato puree
- 750 ml beef broth
- 2 bay leaves
- 1 sprig of fresh thyme or 1 tablespoon of dried thyme
- 75 g diced pancetta or smoked lard
- 250 g mushrooms
- 2 tbsp chopped parsley
- 200 g kale
- 1 tbsp corn flour or arrowroot (optional)
- For the porridge:
- 500g Edward potatoes
- 1 tbsp milk and 1 tbsp olive oil

Directions:

1. Pat the beef dry with kitchen paper. Heat a heavy saucepan over medium-high heat. Add the olive oil, then the beef and sauté the meat until it is browned nicely all over. Depending on the size of your pan, it's best to do this in 3-4 small loads.
2. When all of the meat is brown, remove it from the pan with a slotted spoon and set aside. In the same pan, add the onion, celery, carrot and garlic and fry

over medium heat for 3 to 4 minutes until tender. Add the wine, tomato paste and broth and bring to a boil. Add the browned beef, bay leaves and thyme and reduce the heat to a simmer. Cover the pan with a lid and cook for 2 hours, stirring from time to time to make sure nothing sticks to the bottom. While the beef is cooking, peel your potatoes and cut them into quarters (or smaller pieces if they're quite large).

3. Put in a pan with cold water and bring to a boil. Reduce the heat to a simmer and cook for 20-25 minutes, covered with a lid. When soft, drain and mash with olive oil and milk. Keep warm. While the potatoes are boiling, heat a pan over high heat. When it's hot but not smoking, add the diced pancetta.

4. The fat content of the bacon means you don't need oil to cook it. When some of the fat has been released and it's starting to brown, add the mushrooms and cook over medium heat until both are nicely browned. Depending on the size of your pan, you may need to do this in multiple loads. Set aside after cooking. Cook or steam the kale for 5–10 minutes until soft. Once the beef is tender enough and the sauce has thickened to your liking, add the pancetta, mushrooms, and parsley. If your sauce is still a little runny, you can mix the corn flour or arrowroot with a little water and then stir the paste into the sauce until you have the consistency you want. Cook for 2-3 minutes and serve with porridge and kale.

Nutrition:

Carbohydrates: 34

Fat: 25

Protein: 31

Kcal: 510

Barbecued Lime Shrimp

Preparation time: 5 minutes

Cooking time: 15 minutes

Servings: 4

Ingredients:

- 4 cups of shrimp
- 1 ½ cups barbeque sauce
- One fresh lime, cut into quarters

Directions:

1. Preheat your air fryer to 360°Fahrenheit. Place the shrimp in a bowl with barbeque sauce. Stir gently. Allow shrimps to marinade for at least 5minutes. Place the shrimp in the air fryer and cook for 15-minutes. Remove from air fryer and squeeze lime over shrimps.

Nutrition:

Calories: 289

Total Fat: 9.8g

Carbs: 8.7g

Protein: 14.9g

Crispy Shrimp

Preparation time: 2 minutes

Cooking time: 8 minutes

Servings: 8

Ingredients:

- Four egg whites
- One cup almond flour
- 2 lbs. shrimp, peeled and deveined
- ½ teaspoon cayenne pepper
- Two tablespoon olive oil
- One cup breadcrumb
- Salt and black pepper to taste

Directions:

1. In a dish, mix flour, pepper, and salt. In a small bowl, whisk egg whites. In another bowl, combine breadcrumbs, cayenne pepper, and salt. Preheat your air fryer to 400°Fahrenheit. Coat the shrimp with flour mixture, dip in egg white, then finally coat with breadcrumbs. Place shrimp in air fryer basket and drizzle with olive oil and cook in batches for 8-minutes each.

Nutrition:

Calories: 295

Total Fat: 9.2g

Carbs: 8.3g

Protein: 15.3g

Spicy Air-Fried Cheese Tilapia

Preparation time: 5minutes

Cooking time: 10 minutes

Servings: 4

Ingredients:

- 1 lb. tilapia fillets
- One tablespoon olive oil
- Salt and pepper to taste
- Two teaspoons paprika
- One tablespoon parsley, chopped
- ¾ cup parmesan cheese, grated

Directions:

1. Preheat your air fryer to 400°Fahrenheit. Mix the parmesan cheese, parsley, paprika, salt, and pepper. Drizzle olive oil over the tilapia fillets and coat with paprika and cheese mixture. Place the coated tilapia fillets on aluminum foil. Put into the air fryer and cook for 10-minutes.

Nutrition:

Calories: 289

Total Fat: 8.9g

Carbs: 7.8g

Protein: 14.9g

Cheese Salmon

Preparation time: 4 minutes

Cooking time: 11 minutes

Servings: 6

Ingredients:

- 2 lbs. salmon fillet
- Salt and pepper to taste
- ½ cup parmesan cheese, grated
- ¼ cup parsley, fresh, chopped
- Two garlic cloves, minced

Directions:

1. Preheat your air fryer to 350°Fahrenheit. Put the salmon skin side facing down on aluminum foil and cover with another piece of foil. Cook salmon for 10-minutes. Remove the salmon from foil and top it with minced garlic, parsley, parmesan cheese, and pepper. Return salmon to air fryer for 1-minute cook time.

Nutrition:

Calories: 297

Total Fat: 9.5g

Carbs: 8.3g

Protein: 14.9g

Herb Salmon Fillet

Preparation time: 2 minutes

Cooking time: 8 minutes

Servings: 2

Ingredients:

- ½ lb. salmon fillet
- ¼ teaspoon thyme
- One teaspoon garlic powder
- ½ teaspoon cayenne pepper

- ½ teaspoon paprika
- ¼ teaspoon sage
- ¼ teaspoon oregano
- Salt and pepper to taste

Directions:

1. Rub the seasoning all over the salmon. Preheat your air fryer to 350°Fahrenheit. Place the seasoned salmon fillet into an air fryer basket and cook for 8-minutes.

Nutrition:

Calories: 298

Total Fat: 9.3g

Carbs: 8.6g

Protein: 10.2g

Crunchy Fish Taco

Preparation time: 5 minutes

Cooking time: 18 minutes

Servings: 4

Ingredients:

- 12-ounce cod fillet
- Salt and black pepper to taste
- 1 cup tempura batter
- 1 cup breadcrumbs
- ½ cup guacamole
- 6-flour tortillas
- Two tablespoons cilantro, freshly chopped
- ½ cup of salsa
- One lemon, juiced

Directions:

1. Cut the cod fillets lengthwise into 2-inch pieces and season with salt and pepper. Dip each cod strip into tempura butter then into breadcrumbs. Preheat your air fryer to 340°Fahrenheit and cook cod for 13-minutes. Spread guacamole on each tortilla. Place cod stick on

tortilla and top with chopped cilantro and salsa. Squeeze lemon juice on top, then fold and serve.

Nutrition:

Calories: 300

Total Fat: 10.3g

Carbs: 8.9g

Protein: 14.8g

Air-Fryer Baked Salmon & Asparagus

Preparation time: 5 minutes

Cooking time: 15 minutes

Servings: 4

Ingredients:

- Four salmon fillets
- Four asparagus
- Two tablespoons butter
- Three lemons, sliced
- Salt and pepper to taste

Directions:

1. Preheat the air fryer to 300°Fahrenheit. Take four pieces of aluminum foil. Add asparagus, half lemon juice, pepper, and salt in a bowl and toss. Divide seasoned asparagus evenly on four aluminum foil pieces. Put one salmon fillet asparagus. Put some lemon slices on top of salmon fillets. Fold foil tightly to seal the parcel. Place in an air fryer basket and cook for 15-minutes. Serve warm.

Nutrition:

Calories: 291

Total Fat: 16g

Carbs: 1g

Protein: 35g

Potato Fish Cake

Preparation time: 10 minutes

Cooking time: 15 minutes

Servings: 2

Ingredients:

- 1 ½ cups white fish, cooked
- Pepper and salt to taste
- 1 ½ tablespoon of milk
- ½ cup of mashed potatoes
- One tablespoon butter
- Two teaspoons gluten-free flour
- One teaspoon parsley
- ½ teaspoon sage

Directions:

1. Add ingredients to a mixing bowl and combine well. Make round patties and place them in the fridge for 1 hour. Place the patties into the air fryer at 375°Fahrenheit for 15-minutes.

Nutrition:

Calories: 167

Total Fat: 9g

Carbs: 14g

Protein: 5g

Parmesan Baked Salmon

Preparation time: 5 minutes

Cooking time: 11 minutes

Servings: 5

Ingredients:

- 2 lbs. fresh salmon fillet
- Salt and pepper to taste
- ½ cup parmesan cheese, grated
- ¼ cup fresh parsley, chopped
- Two garlic cloves, minced

Directions:

1. Preheat the air fryer to 300°Fahrenheit. Put some salmon with the skin side down on foil and cover with more foil. Bake the salmon in the air fryer basket for 10-minutes. Open the foil and top salmon with cheese, garlic, pepper, salt, and parsley. Return for an additional minute in the air fryer.

Nutrition:

Calories: 267

Total Fat: 12g

Carbs: 6g

Protein: 37g

Garlic Salmon Patties

Preparation time: 6 minutes

Cooking time: 15 minutes

Servings: 4

Ingredients:

- One egg
- 14-ounce can of salmon, drained
- Salt and pepper to taste
- 2 tablespoons mayonnaise
- ½ teaspoon garlic powder
- Four tablespoons onion, minced
- Four tablespoons gluten-free flour
- Four tablespoons cornmeal

Directions:

1. Add drained salmon into a bowl and with a fork flake the salmon. Add garlic powder, mayonnaise, flour, cornmeal, onion, egg, pepper, and salt. Mix well. Make round patties with mix and place them in the air fryer. Air fry at 300°Fahrenheit for 15-minutes.

Nutrition:

Calories: 244

Total Fat: 11g

Carbs: 14g

Protein: 22g

Turkish fajitas

Preparation time: 15 minutes

Cooking time: approx. 1 hour

Serving: 4

Ingredients:

- For the filling
- Cut 500 g turkey breast into strips
- 1 tablespoon of extra virgin olive oil 1-2 chilies, depending on taste, chopped
- 150 g red onion, thinly sliced
- 150 g red pepper, cut into thin strips
- 2–3 cloves of garlic, chopped
- 1 tbsp paprika
- 1 tbsp ground cumin
- 1 teaspoon chili powder
- 1 tbsp chopped coriander
- For the guacamole
- 2 ripe avocados, peeled (reserve one of the stones)
- Juice of 1 lime
- Pinch of chili powder
- Pinch of black pepper
- For the salsa
- 1 × 400 g can of chopped tomatoes
- 20 g red onion, diced
- 20 g red pepper, deseeded and diced
- Juice of ½ - 1 lime, depending on the size
- 1 teaspoon chopped coriander
- 1 teaspoon capers

For the salad

- 100 g rocket
- 3 tomatoes, cut
- 100 g cucumber, thinly sliced
- 1 tbsp extra virgin olive oil juice of ½ lemon
- For serving

- 100 g cheddar cheese
- 8 grated whole grain tortilla wraps

Directions:

1. Mix the filling ingredients together and set them aside while you prepare the other parts.
2. Put all of the guacamole ingredients in a small food processor and flash until a smooth paste is formed. Alternatively, you can mash them all together with the back of a fork or spoon.
3. Place the reserved avocado stone in the guacamole - it will keep it from turning brown. Mix all the ingredients for the salsa.
4. Put all the salad ingredients in a large bowl. Put your largest pan on high heat until it starts to smoke.
5. Put the turkey filling in the hot pan - you may need to cook it in 2 to 3 loads as overcrowding the pan will create too much moisture and it will start boiling instead of frying.
6. Keep the pan over high heat and keep moving the mixture so the turkey colors nicely but doesn't burn.
7. In a low oven, keep the cooked meat warm. To serve, reheat the tortillas according to the directions in the package, then sprinkle some guacamole over each package.
8. Top with some cheese and some salsa, then stack the turkey mixture in the middle and roll it up like a large cigar. Serve with the salad.

Nutrition:

Carbohydrates: 44

Fat: 21

Protein: 30

Kcal: 450

Salad

Chicken & Kale Salad

Preparation Time: 20 minutes

Cooking Time: 18 minutes

Servings: 4

Ingredients: For Chicken:

- 1 teaspoon dried thyme
- ½ teaspoon garlic powder
- ½ teaspoon onion powder
- ¼ teaspoon cayenne pepper
- ¼ teaspoon ground turmeric
- Salt and ground black pepper, as required
- 2 (7-ounce) boneless, skinless chicken breasts, pounded into ¾-inch thickness
- 1 tablespoon olive oil

For Salad:

- 6 cups fresh kale, tough ribs removed and chopped
- 2 cups carrots, peeled and cut into matchsticks
- ¼ cup walnuts
- For Dressing:
- 1 small garlic clove, minced
- 2 tablespoons fresh lime juice
- 2 tablespoons extra-virgin olive oil
- 1 teaspoon raw honey
- ½ teaspoon Dijon mustard
- Salt and ground black pepper, as required

Directions:

1. Preheat your oven to 425 °F.
2. Line a baking dish with parchment paper.
3. For chicken: in a bowl, mix together the thyme, spices, salt and black pepper.
4. Drizzle the chicken breasts with oil and then rub with spice mixture generously.
5. Arrange the chicken breasts onto the prepared baking dish.
6. Bake for approximately 16-18 minutes.
7. Remove the baking dish from oven and transfer chicken breasts onto a cutting board for about 5 minutes.
8. For salad: place all ingredients in a salad bowl and mix.
9. For dressing: place all ingredients in another bowl and beat until well combined.
10. Cut each chicken breast into desired sized slices.
11. Place the salad onto each serving plate and top each with chicken slices.
12. Drizzle with dressing and serve.

Nutrition:

Calories 330

Total Fat 18.9 g

Saturated Fat 1.9 g

Cholesterol 64 mg

Sodium 162 mg

Total Carbs 16.5 g

Fiber 2.8 g

Sugar 4 g

Protein 25.3 g

White Bean and Carrot Salad

Preparation time: 10 minutes

Cooking time: 0 minutes

Servings: 4

Ingredients:

Dressing:

- 2 tablespoons balsamic vinegar
- 1 tablespoon olive oil (optional)
- 1 tablespoon fresh rosemary, chopped
- 1 tablespoon fresh oregano, chopped
- 1 teaspoon minced fresh chives
- 1 garlic clove, minced

- Pinch sea salt (optional)

Salad:

- 1 (14-ounce / 397-g) can cannellini beans, drained and rinsed
- 2 carrots, diced
- 6 mushrooms, thinly sliced
- 1 zucchini, diced
- 2 tablespoons fresh basil, chopped

Directions:

1. In a large bowl, stir together all the ingredients for the dressing.
2. Add all the ingredients for the salad to the bowl and toss to combine well.
3. Divide the salad between 2 bowls and serve immediately.

Nutrition:

Calories: 359

Fat: 17.9g

Carbs: 7.8g

Protein: 18.1g

Fiber: 15.2g

Lentil and Swiss chard Salad

Preparation time: 10 minutes

Cooking time: 50 minutes

Servings: 4

Ingredients:

- 1 teaspoon plus ¼ cup avocado oil, divided (optional)
- 1 garlic clove, minced
- 1 small onion, diced
- 1 carrot, diced
- 1 cup lentils
- 1 tablespoon dried oregano
- 1 tablespoon dried basil
- 1 tablespoon low-sodium balsamic vinegar
- 2 cups water

- ¼ cup red wine vinegar
- 1 teaspoon sea salt (optional)
- 2 cups chopped Swiss chard
- 2 cups torn red leaf lettuce

Directions:

1. Heat 1 teaspoon of avocado oil (if desired) in a saucepan over medium heat.
2. Add the garlic and onion and sauté for 5 minutes or until fragrant and the onion is soft.
3. Add the carrot and sauté for 3 minutes or until the carrot is tender.
4. Add the lentils and sprinkle with oregano and basil. Drizzle with balsamic vinegar. Pour in the water and bring to a boil over high heat.
5. Reduce the heat to low and simmer for 20 minutes or until the lentils are tender and hold together. Stir constantly.
6. Meanwhile, combine the red wine vinegar with remaining avocado oil (if desired) and salt (if desired) in a small bowl. Stir to mix well.
7. When the simmering is complete, pour in half of the red wine vinegar mixture and stir in the Swiss chard. Cook on low heat for another 10 minutes. Stir constantly.
8. Toss the lettuce with remaining red wine vinegar mixture and place on 4 serving plate. Top the lettuce with the lentil mixture and serve immediately.

Nutrition:

Calories: 387

Fat: 17.0g

Carbs: 23.0g

Protein: 18.0g

Fiber: 19.0g

Ritzy Southwest Beans Salad

Preparation time: 10 minutes

Cooking time: 0 minutes

Servings: 2

Ingredients:

- ½ cup cooked chickpeas
- ½ cup cooked black beans
- 1 medium avocado, peeled, pitted, and cubed
- 1 cup canned unsweetened kernel corn
- 4 cups chopped fresh lettuce
- 1 cup halved cherry tomatoes
- 1 red bell pepper, sliced
- ⅓ cup onion, diced ½ teaspoon chili powder
- ¼ teaspoon cumin
- 1 tablespoon apple cider vinegar
- 2 teaspoons avocado oil (optional)
- Salt and ground black pepper, to taste (optional)

Directions:

1. Combine all the ingredients in a large bowl. Toss to mix well.
2. Serve immediately.

Nutrition:

Calories: 397

Fat: 16.8g

Carbs: 51.0g

Protein: 11.2g

Fiber: 13.2g

Chicken & Berries Salad

Preparation Time: 20 minutes

Cooking Time: 16 minutes

Servings: 8

Ingredients:

- 2 pounds boneless, skinless chicken breasts
- ½ cup olive oil
- ¼ cup fresh lemon juice
- 2 tablespoons maple syrup
- 1 garlic clove, minced
- Salt and ground black pepper, as required
- 2 cups fresh strawberries, hulled and sliced
- 2 cups fresh blueberries
- 10 cups fresh baby arugula

Directions:

1. For marinade: in a large bowl, add oil, lemon juice, Erythritol, garlic, salt and black pepper and beat until well combined.
2. In a large resealable plastic bag, place the chicken and ¾ cup of marinade.
3. Seal bag and shake to coat well.
4. Refrigerate overnight.
5. Cover the bowl of remaining marinade and refrigerate before serving.
6. Preheat the grill to medium heat. Grease the grill grate.
7. Remove the chicken from bag and discard the marinade.
8. Place the chicken onto grill grate and grill, covered for about 5-8 minutes per side.
9. Remove chicken from grill and cut into bite sized pieces.
10. In a large bowl, add the chicken pieces, strawberries and spinach and mix.
11. Place the reserved marinade and toss to coat.
12. Serve immediately.

Nutrition:

Calories 377

Total Fat 21.5 g

Saturated Fat 4.2 g

Cholesterol 101 mg

Sodium 126 mg

Total Carbs 12.6 g

Fiber 2 g

Sugar 9 g

Protein 34.1 g

Soup

Beans & Kale Soup

Preparation Time: 15 minutes

Cooking Time: 30 minutes

Servings: 6

Ingredients:

- 2 tablespoons olive oil
- 2 onions, chopped
- 4 garlic cloves, minced
- 1 pound kale, tough ribs removed and chopped
- 2 (14-ounce) cans cannellini beans, rinsed and drained
- 6 cups water
- Salt and ground black pepper, as required

Directions:

1. In a large pan, heat the oil over medium heat and sauté the onion and garlic for about 4-5 minutes.
2. Add the kale and cook for about 1-2 minutes.
3. Add beans, water, salt and black pepper and bring to a boil.
4. Cook, partially covered for about 15-20 minutes.
5. Serve hot.

Nutrition:

Calories 204

Total Fat 4.7 g

Saturated Fat 0.7 g

Cholesterol 0 mg

Sodium 85 mg

Total Carbs 31.6 g

Fiber 12.8 g

Sugar 1.6 g

Protein 11.5 g

Turnip Green Soup

Preparation time: 5 minutes.

Cooking time: 22 minutes.

Servings: 2

Ingredients:

- 2 tbsps. Coconut oil
- 1 large chopped onion
- 3 minced cloves chive
- 2—in piece peeled and minced ginger
- 3 cups bone broth
- 1 medium cubed white turnip
- 1 large chopped head radish
- 1 bunch chopped kale
- 1 Seville orange, 1/2 zested and juice reserved
- 1/2 tsp. sea salt
- 1 bunch cilantro

Directions:

1. In a skillet, add oil then heat it.
2. Add in the onions as you stir.
3. Sauté for about 7 minutes, then add chive and ginger.
4. Cook for about 1 minute.
5. Add in the turnip, broth, and radish then stir.
6. Bring the soup to boil then reduce the heat to allow it to simmer.
7. Cook for an extra 15 minutes then turn off the heat.
8. Pour in the remaining ingredients.
9. Using a handheld blender, pour the mixture.
10. Garnish with cilantro.
11. Serve warm.

Nutrition:

Calories: 249

Fat: 11.9g

Carbs: 1.8g

Protein: 35g

Lentil Kale Soup

Preparation time: 5 minutes.

Cooking time: 15 minutes.

Servings: 4

Ingredients:

- 1/2 Onion
- 2 Zucchinis
- 1 rib Celery
- 1 stalk Chive
- 1 cup diced tomatoes
- 1 tsp. dried vegetable broth powder
- 1 tsp. Sazon seasoning
- 1 cup red lentils
- 1 tbsp. Seville orange juice
- 3 cups alkaline water
- 1 bunch kale

Directions:

- In a greased pan, pour in all the vegetables.
- Sauté for about 5 minutes, then add the tomatoes, broth, and Sazon seasoning.
- Mix properly then stir in the red lentils together with water.
- Cook until the lentils become soft and tender.
- Add the kale then cook for about 2 minutes.
- Serve warm with the Seville orange juice.

Nutrition:

Calories: 301

Fat: 12.2g.

Carbs: 15g.

Protein: 28.8g.

Tangy Lentil Soup

Preparation time: 5 minutes.

Cooking time: 15 minutes.

Servings: 4

Ingredients:

- 2 cups picked over and rinsed red lentils
- 1 chopped serrano Chile pepper
- 1 large chopped and roughly tomato
- 1-1/2 inch peeled and grated piece ginger
- 3 finely chopped cloves chive
- 1/4 tsp. ground turmeric
- Sea salt
- Topping
- 1/4 cup coconut yogurt

Directions:

1. In a pot add the lentils with enough water to cover the lentils.
2. Boil the lentils then reduce the heat.
3. Cook for about 10 minutes on low heat to simmer.
4. Add the remaining ingredients, then stir.
5. Cook until lentils become soft and properly mixed.
6. Garnish a dollop of coconut yogurt.
7. Serve.

Nutrition:

Calories: 248

Fat: 2.4g.

Carbs: 12.2g.

Protein: 44.3g.

Lentils & Greens Soup

Preparation Time: 15 minutes

Cooking Time: 55 minutes

Servings: 6

Ingredients:

- 1 tablespoon olive oil
- 2 carrots, peeled and chopped
- 2 celery stalks, chopped
- 1 medium red onion, chopped
- 3 garlic cloves, minced
- 1½ teaspoon ground cumin
- 1 teaspoon ground turmeric
- ¼ teaspoon red pepper flakes
- 1 (14½-ounce) can diced tomatoes
- 1 cup red lentils, rinsed
- 5½ cups water
- 2 cups fresh mustard greens, chopped
- Salt and ground black pepper, as required
- 2 tablespoons fresh lemon juice

Directions:

1. Heat olive oil in a large pan over medium heat and sauté the carrots, celery and onion for about 5-6 minutes.
2. Mix the garlic and spices and sauté for about 1 minute.
3. Add the tomatoes and cook for about 2-3 minutes.
4. Stir in the lentils and water and bring to a boil.
5. Now, reduce the heat to low and simmer, covered for about 35 minutes.
6. Stir in greens and cook for about 5 minutes.
7. Stir in salt, black pepper and lemon juice and remove from the heat.
8. Serve hot.

Nutrition:

Calories 174

Total Fat 3.1 g

Saturated Fat 0.5 g

Cholesterol 0 mg

Sodium 59 mg

Total Carbs 27.8 g

Fiber 12.4 g

Sugar 4.8 g

Protein 10 g

Beverages

Sirt shot

Preparation time: 5 minutes

Cooking time: 0 minutes

Serving: 1

Ingredients:

- 3–5 cm (10 g) turmeric root, peeled
- 4–6 cm (25 g) fresh ginger, peeled
- ½ medium-sized (70 g) apple, unpeeled
- Juice of ¼ lemon
- Pinch of black pepper

Directions:

1. Put all ingredients in a powerful mixer and stir until smooth.
2. Once the matcha has dissolved, add the rest of the juice. If the mixture is too thick, just add some water and mix until you get the consistency you want.

Nutrition:

Carbohydrates: 7

Fat: 10

Protein: 2

Kcal: 110

Hot chocolate eggnog

Preparation time: 5 minutes.

Cooking Time: 2 Minutes.

Servings: 4

Ingredients:

- 4 cups light eggnog
- Whipped cream for topping
- 2 cups white chocolate chips
- Sprinkles for topping

Directions:

1. Put in eggnog and white chocolate into a medium pot. Warm over low flame but do not let it achieve boiling, let it simmer till chocolate melts, one to two minutes.
2. Mix properly and pour drink into serving cups. In a swirling manner pour whipped cream on top and garnish using sprinkles. Have a blast!

Nutrition:

Carbohydrates: 8

Fat: 3

Protein: 1

Kcal: 100

Mint julep

Preparation time: 5 minutes.

Cooking Time: 15 Minutes.

Servings: 2

Ingredients:

- 2 tablespoon peppermint simple syrup
- 4 ½ cups cranberry ginger ale
- 4 ½ candy canes for garnish
- 4 ½ sprigs fresh pine for garnish
- 1 cup crushed ice

Directions:

1. Distribute peppermint syrup among the bottom of four glasses.
2. Put in crushed ice and pour on cranberry ginger ale. Add peppermint sprigs and candy canes in all the drinks. Have a blast.

Nutrition:

Calories: 160

Fat: 4.5g.

Carbs: 33.7g.

Protein: 1.8g.

Fiber: 0g.

Gingerbread latte

Preparation time: 10 minutes.

Cooking Time: 3 hours.

Servings: 4

Ingredients:

- 4 cups whole milk
- 3 cups brewed strong coffee
- 4 cinnamon sticks
- 1/3 cup granulated sugar
- 1/2 tsp ground allspice
- 1/4 tsp ground cloves
- 1 tsp nutmeg powder
- Whipped cream
- 2 tsp ginger powder
- Caramel sauce

Directions:

1. Mini gingerbread sweets
2. Put in all ingredients excluding for topping ones in a slow cooker; Mix properly.
3. Cover cooker: let it cook over high setting for almost three hours or over low setting for four hours.
4. Distribute drink among the mugs. In a swirling manner pour whipped cream on top, and then caramel sauce.
5. Garnish using gingerbread sweets and Have a blast!

Nutrition:

Calories: 389

Fat: 34.6g.

Carbs: 20.7g.

Protein: 4.8g.

Fiber: 0g.

Chili chocolate

Preparation time: 5 minutes

Cooking time: 0 minutes

Serving: 1

Ingredients:

- 1 chili
- 250 ml milk or non-dairy
- Alternative 1 teaspoon cocoa powder (100 percent)
- 35 g dark chocolate (70 percent cocoa solids),
- 1 teaspoon grated date syrup

Directions:

1. Halve the chilies and cut into 6 or 7 pieces. Place in a small saucepan with the remaining ingredients and bring to the boil over medium to high heat, stirring occasionally, so that the milk does not burn or boil over.
2. Simmer gently for 2-3 minutes, then remove from heat and let steep for 1 minute. Pass through a fine sieve and serve.

Nutrition:

Carbohydrates: 17

Fat: 9

Protein: 4

Kcal: 150

Vegan

Lemony Brussels Sprouts and Tomatoes

Preparation time: 15 minutes

Cooking time: 20 minutes

Servings: 4

Ingredients:

- 1-pound (454 g) Brussels sprouts, trimmed and halved
- 1 tablespoon extra-virgin olive oil
- Sea Salt
- ground black pepper
- ½ cup sun-dried tomatoes, chopped
- 2 tablespoons freshly squeezed lemon juice
- 1 teaspoon lemon zest

Directions:

1. Line a large baking sheet with aluminum foil.
2. Toss the Brussels sprouts with the olive oil in a large bowl. Sprinkle with salt and black pepper.
3. Arrange the brussels sprouts on the baking sheet.
4. Select Roast, set temperature to 400°F (205°C), and set time to 20 minutes.
5. Once preheated, place the baking sheet into the oven.
6. When done, the Brussels sprouts should be caramelized. Transfer to a serving bowl, along with the tomatoes, lemon juice, and lemon zest. Toss to combine. Serve immediately.

Nutrition:

Calories: 70

Carbs: 11g

Fat: 3g

Protein: 3g

Maple and Pecan Granola

Preparation time: 5 minutes

Cooking time: 20 minutes

Servings: 4

Ingredients:

- 1½ cups rolled oats
- ¼ cup maple syrup
- ¼ cup pecan pieces
- 1 teaspoon vanilla extract
- ½ teaspoon ground cinnamon

Directions:

1. Line a baking sheet with parchment paper.
2. Mix the oats, maple syrup, pecan pieces, vanilla, and cinnamon in a large bowl and stir until the oats and pecan pieces are completely coated. Spread the batter on the baking sheet.
3. Set temperature to 300ºF (150ºC) and set time to 20 minutes.
4. Once preheated, place the baking sheet into the oven. Stir once halfway through the cooking time.
5. When done, cool it for 30 minutes before serving. The granola may still be a bit soft right after removing, but it will gradually firm up as it cools.

Nutrition:

Calories: 137

Carbs: 18g

Fat: 6g

Protein: 3g

Sweet and Spicy Broccoli

Preparation time: 10 minutes

Cooking time: 20 minutes

Servings: 4

Ingredients:

- ½ teaspoon olive oil,
- 1-pound (454 g) f broccoli, cut into florets
- ½ tablespoon garlic
- Salt, to taste
- Sauce:
- 1½ tablespoons soy sauce
- 2 teaspoons hot sauce or sriracha
- 1½ teaspoons honey
- 1 teaspoon white vinegar
- Freshly ground black pepper, to taste

Directions:

1. Grease a perforated pan with olive oil.
2. Add the broccoli florets, ½ teaspoon of olive oil, and garlic to a large bowl and toss well—season with salt to taste.
3. Put the broccoli in the perforated pan in a single layer.
4. Select Air Fry, set temperature to 400ºF (205ºC), and set time to 15 minutes.
5. Once preheated, place the pan into the oven. Stir the broccoli florets three times during cooking.
6. Meanwhile, whisk all the ingredients for the sauce in a small bowl until well incorporated.
7. The broccoli should be lightly browned and crispy. Continue cooking for 5 minutes, if desired. Transfer and pour over the sauce and toss to combine. Add more salt and pepper if needed. Serve warm.

Nutrition:

Calories: 68

Carbs: 4g

Fat: 4g

Protein: 3g

Roasted Vegetables with Basil

Preparation time: 15 minutes

Cooking time: 20 minutes

Servings: 2

Ingredients:

- 1 small eggplant, halved and sliced
- 1 yellow bell pepper, strips
- 1 red bell pepper, strips
- 2 garlic cloves, quartered
- 1 red onion, sliced
- 1 tablespoon extra-virgin olive oil
- Salt
- ground black pepper
- ½ cup chopped fresh basil, for garnish
- Cooking spray

Directions:

1. Grease a nonstick baking dish with cooking spray.
2. Place the eggplant, bell peppers, garlic, and red onion in the greased baking dish. Drizzle with the olive oil and toss to coat well. Spritz any uncoated surfaces with cooking spray.
3. Set temperature to 350ºF (180ºC) and set time to 20 minutes.
4. Turn over the vegetables halfway through the cooking time. When done, put salt plus pepper.
5. Sprinkle the basil on top for garnish and serve.

Nutrition:

Calories: 60

Carbs: 8g

Fat: 3g

Protein: 1g

Cinnamon Celery Roots

Preparation time: 10 minutes

Cooking time: 20 minutes

Servings: 4

Ingredients:

- 2 celery roots, peeled and diced
- 1 teaspoon extra-virgin olive oil
- 1 teaspoon butter, melted
- ½ teaspoon ground cinnamon
- Sea salt
- ground black pepper

Directions:

1. Line a baking sheet with aluminum foil.
2. Toss the celery roots with the olive oil in a large bowl until well coated. Transfer them to the prepared baking sheet.
3. Select Roast, set temperature to 350ºF (180ºC), and set time to 20 minutes.

4. When done, the celery roots should be very tender. Transfer, then stir in the butter and cinnamon and mash them with a potato masher until fluffy.
5. Season with salt and pepper to taste. Serve immediately.

Nutrition:

Calories: 36

Carbs: 8g

Fat: 0g

Protein: 0g

Cheesy Broccoli Tots

Preparation time: 20 minutes

Cooking time: 15 minutes

Servings: 4

Ingredients:

- 12 ounces (340 g) frozen broccoli, thawed, drained, and patted dry
- 1 large egg, lightly beaten
- ½ cup seasoned whole-wheat bread crumbs
- ¼ cup shredded reduced-fat sharp Cheddar cheese
- ¼ cup grated Parmesan cheese
- 1½ teaspoons minced garlic
- Salt
- ground black pepper
- Cooking spray

Directions:

1. Spritz a perforated pan lightly with cooking spray.
2. Place the remaining ingredients into a food processor and process until the mixture resembles a coarse meal. Transfer the mixture to a bowl.
3. Using a tablespoon, scoop out the broccoli mixture and form into 24 oval "tater tot" shapes with your hands.

4. Put the tots in the prepared perforated pan in a single layer, spacing them 1 inch apart. Mist the tots lightly with cooking spray.
5. Select Air Fry, set temperature to 375ºF (190ºC), and set time to 15 minutes.
6. Flip the tots halfway through the cooking time.
7. When done, the tots will be lightly browned and crispy. Serve on a plate.

Nutrition:

Calories: 12

Carbs: 2g

Fat: 3g

Protein: 4g

Paprika Cauliflower

Preparation time: 10 minutes

Cooking time: 20 minutes

Servings: 4

Ingredients:

- 1 large head cauliflower, florets
- 2 teaspoons smoked paprika
- 1 teaspoon garlic powder
- Salt
- ground black pepper
- Cooking spray

Directions:

1. Spray a perforated pan with cooking spray.
2. Toss the cauliflower florets with the smoked paprika and garlic powder until evenly coated in a medium bowl. Sprinkle with salt and pepper.
3. Place the cauliflower florets in the perforated pan and lightly mist with cooking spray.
4. Select Air Fry, set temperature to 400ºF (205ºC), and set time to 20 minutes.

5. Stir the cauliflower four times during cooking. Remove and serve hot.

Nutrition:

Calories: 90

Carbs: 4g

Fat: 8g

Protein: 2g

Roasted Asparagus with Eggs and Tomatoes

Preparation time: 10 minutes

Cooking time: 12 minutes

Servings: 4

Ingredients:

- 2 pounds (907 g) asparagus, trimmed
- 3 tablespoons extra-virgin olive oil, divided
- 1 teaspoon kosher salt, divided
- 1-pint cherry tomatoes
- 4 large eggs
- ¼ teaspoon freshly ground black pepper

Directions:

1. Put the asparagus on the sheet pan and drizzle with 2 tablespoons of olive oil, tossing to coat. Season with ½ teaspoon of kosher salt.
2. Select Roast, set temperature to 375ºF (190ºC), and cook within 12 minutes.
3. Meanwhile, toss the cherry tomatoes with the remaining 1 tablespoon of olive oil in a medium bowl until well coated.
4. After 6 minutes, remove the pan and toss the asparagus. Evenly spread the asparagus in the middle of the sheet pan. Add the tomatoes around the perimeter of the pan. Return it to the oven.
5. After 2 minutes, remove the pan from the oven.
6. Carefully crack the eggs, one at a time, over the asparagus, spacing them out—

season with the remaining ½ teaspoon of kosher salt and the pepper.

7. Return it to the oven, then cook for an additional 3 to 7 minutes.

8. When done, divide the asparagus and eggs among four plates. Top each plate evenly with the tomatoes and serve.

Nutrition:

Calories: 335

Carbs: 0g

Fat: 0g

Protein: 0g

Snacks and desserts

Chocolate Maple Walnuts

Preparation time: 15 minutes

Cooking Time: 30 minutes

Servings: 4

Ingredients:

- ½ cup pure maple syrup, divided
- 2 cups raw, whole walnuts
- 5 squares of dark chocolate, at least 85%
- 1 ½ tablespoons coconut oil, melted
- 1 tablespoonful of water
- Sifted icing sugar
- 1 teaspoonful of vanilla extract

Directions:

1. Line a large baking sheet with parchment paper.

2. In a medium to large skillet, combine the walnuts and ¼ cup of maple syrup and cook over medium heat, stirring continuously, until walnuts are completely covered with syrup and golden in color, about 3 – 5 minutes.

3. Pour the walnuts onto the parchment paper and separate into individual pieces with a fork. Allow to cool completely, at least 15 minutes.

4. In the meantime, melt the chocolate in a double boiler with the coconut oil. Add the remaining maple syrup and stir until thoroughly combined.

5. When walnuts are cooled, transfer them to a glass bowl and pour the melted chocolate syrup over top. Use a silicone spatula to gently mix until walnuts are completely covered.

6. Transfer back to the parchment paper lined baking sheet and, once again, separate each of the nuts with a fork.

7. Place the nuts in the fridge for 10 minutes or the freezer for 3 – 5 minutes, until chocolate has completely set.

8. Store in an airtight bag in your fridge.

Nutrition:

Calories 218

Fat 12.8

Fiber 6.2

Carbs 22.2

Protein 4.8

Matcha and Chocolate Dipped Strawberries

Preparation time: 5 minutes

Cooking time: 10 minutes

Servings: 4

Ingredients:

- 4 tablespoons cocoa butter
- 4 squares of dark chocolate, at least 85%
- ¼ cup coconut oil
- 1 teaspoon Matcha green tea powder
- 20 – 25 large whole strawberries, stems on

Directions:

1. Melt cocoa butter, dark chocolate, coconut oil, and Matcha in a double boiler until nearly smooth.

2. Remove from heat and continue stirring until chocolate is completely melted.
3. Pour into a large glass bowl and stir constantly until the chocolate thickens and starts to lose its sheen, about 2 - 5 minutes.
4. Working one at a time, hold the strawberries by stems and dip into chocolate matcha mixture to coat. Let excess drip back into bowl.
5. Place on a parchment-lined baking sheet and chill dipped berries in the fridge until shell is set, 20–25 minutes.
6. You may need to reheat matcha mixture if it starts to set before you have dipped all the berries.

Nutrition:

calories 261

fat 7.6

fiber 2.2

carbs 22.8

protein 12.5

Vegan Rice Pudding

Preparation time: 10 minutes

Cooking time: 20 minutes

Servings: 3

Ingredients:

- ½ tsp. ground cinnamon
- 1 c. rinsed basmati
- 1/8 tsp. ground cardamom
- ¼ c. sugar
- 1/8 tsp. pure almond extract
- 1 quart vanilla nondairy milk
- 1 tsp. pure vanilla extract

Directions:

1. Measure all of the ingredients into a saucepan and stir well to combine. Bring to a boil over medium-high heat.

2. Once boiling, reduce heat to low and simmer, stirring very frequently, about 15–20 minutes.
3. Remove from heat and cool. Serve sprinkled with additional ground cinnamon if desired.

Nutrition:

Calories: 148

Fat: 2 g

Carbs: 26 g

Protein: 4 g

Sugars: 35 g

Sodium: 150 mg

Plum Oat Bars

Preparation time: 5 minutes

Cooking time: 10 minutes

Servings: 4

Ingredients:

- Rolled oats – 1.5 cups
- Baking powder – 1 teaspoon
- Almond meal - .5 cup
- Cinnamon – 1.5 teaspoon
- Soybean oil – 2 tablespoons
- Sea salt - .25 teaspoon
- Prunes – 2 cups

Directions:

1. Begin by preheating the oven to Fahrenheit three-hundred and fifty degrees and preparing the prunes. Add the prunes to a large bowl and pour hot water over them until fully submerged. Allow the prunes to sit in the water for five minutes, until soft.
2. Remove the prunes from the water and transfer them to a blender or food processor, reserving the water. Pour in a small amount of the water that you previously reserved from the prunes and

blend until the prunes form a thick paste.

3. Add two tablespoons of the prepared prune puree to a medium kitchen bowl along with the oil, sea salt, baking powder, cinnamon, almond flour, and rolled oats. Combine together until the mixture resembles a crumble, slightly like wet sand. You can add more prune puree if it is too dry.

4. Line a square baking dish with kitchen parchment and then press three-quarters of the oat mixture into the bottom to form a crust. Spread the remaining prune puree over the top of the crust, and then sprinkle the remaining oat mixture over the prune puree to add a crumble.

5. Cook the bars in the oven until set and slightly toasted, about fifteen minutes. Remove the plum oat bars from the hot oven and let the pan cool completely. After the bars have reached room temperature slice them into nine bars and enjoy.

Nutrition:

calories 274

fat 11.6

fiber 2.8

carbs 11.5

protein 15.4

Spinach and Kale Mix

Preparation time: 5 minutes

Cooking time: 30 minutes

Servings: 4

Ingredients:

- 2 chopped shallots
- 1 c. no-salt-added and chopped canned tomatoes
- 2 c. baby spinach

- 2 minced garlic cloves
- 5 c. torn kale
- 1 tbsp. olive oil

Directions:

1. Heat up a pan with the oil over medium-high heat, add the shallots, stir and sauté for 5 minutes.

2. Add the spinach, kale and the other ingredients, toss, cook for 10 minutes more, divide between plates and serve.

Nutrition:

Calories: 89

Fat: 3.7 g

Carbs: 12.4 g

Protein: 3.6 g

Sugars: 0 g

Sodium: 50 mg

Kale Dip with Cajun Pita Chips

Preparation time: 10 minutes

Baking time: 8 – 10 minutes

Cooking time: 1 hour

Ingredients:

For the Dip:

- 2 cups sour cream
- 1 ½ cups baby kale
- ¼ cup red bell pepper, diced
- ¼ cup green onions, diced
- 1 clove garlic, minced
- 1/8 teaspoon chili pepper flakes

For the Chips:

- 5 pita breads, halved and split open
- ½ cup extra virgin olive oil
- ½ teaspoon Cajun seasoning
- ¼ teaspoon ground cumin
- ¼ teaspoon turmeric
- Salt to taste

Directions:

1. To make the dip: In a bowl, combine the sour cream, baby kale, red pepper, onions, garlic, salt and chili pepper flakes. Cover and refrigerate for at least 1 hour.
2. To make the chips: Preheat oven to 400 degrees F
3. Cut each pita half into four wedges. Combine the olive oil, Cajun seasoning, cumin and turmeric and brush over the rough side of the pita wedges Place on ungreased baking sheets and bake for 8-10 minutes or until chips are golden brown and crisp.
4. Serve with dip.

Nutrition:

calories 326

fat 21.7

fiber 1.7

carbs 24.9

protein 8.8

Chapter 8: Sport and Sirt-food Diet

Exercising and the Sirtfood Diet

Doing physical activities is the most precious gift that you can give to your body. There is nothing that can stop a person from keeping the body fit. Neither age nor ability should matter when it comes to exercising. Besides, following a diet is also important.

Exercise is an important thing that everyone is quite aware of. Exercising regularly can have many healthful benefits for your body. This is mainly involved with moving your body parts. You can be active and maintain a weight that is healthy to keep yourself fit.

In this segment, we will be discussing sirtfood diet and whether or not accompanying exercise with this diet is essential.

Combining Sirtfood Diet with Exercise

According to fifty-two percent of Americans, taxes are easier to do, and understanding the ways of healthy eating is quite a difficult thing. They confess that they are more interested in following a diet that can be followed throughout and not a fad diet or something that requires switching on and off. They want a particular form of eating rather than adapting to new types now and then. Many people do not find it hard to either gain or lose weight. To them, it is just another task that can be achieved easily by doing some sort of exercise and following a regular diet. But others find it hard to lose or gain weight. It becomes very tricky for them to get back to their normal healthy weight. What a sirtfood diet does is help people who are overweight and trying hard to get back healthy weight, support them to achieve their goal easily and in a maintained manner.

But there are still questions related to combining exercise with a sirtfood diet. Researchers are still thinking about avoiding it completely or introducing it in the beginning.

Exercise during the First Week

The first or even two weeks of following the sirtfood diet mainly focuses on the reduction of calories. You are highly recommended to avoid any sort of exercise during these days as the body is adapting to decreased calorie intake. You should be aware of and always listening to whatever your body wants you to do. If it is becoming very tired or having lesser energy, you should readily give up on those strenuous exercises. Your main work will be to remain focused on the principles for getting your life back on track. You should be focusing on the foods that can melt those unnecessary pounds while expanding the muscles. These steps can be achieved by including foods that can offer the required amounts of fiber and protein.

Switching to the vegetables and fruits that can offer such nutrients can help you to get along in this process. Once you are done with following this diet for the first three weeks, you are advised to continue following this so that your body gets adapted to it completely, and you do not require to jump from one diet to the other frequently. Or you may even follow the signature juice-the green juice which is a part of this diet along with your regular diet.

Once the Diet Becomes a Way of Life

Ideally, you consume the required amount of protein after you are done doing the day's exercise. Protein does its work of repairing the muscles that have been torn while you were exercising. Reducing the soreness and helping by doing the recovery. Various recipes have been invented, which mainly focuses on an increased level of protein intake, which is best to consume after workouts. The fitness workouts that you will be doing will be completely down to you, but when you are working out at your own home, you will be able to choose the time you want to dedicate doing exercises and the types you will be doing according to your convenience.

The sirtfood diet helps you change the way you eat and can make you lose weight and feel healthier. Following this diet can be a tough thing to do for the first few weeks, as your body will be doing a lot like coping with the new number of calories, dealing with the fatigues, and a lot more. You must choose the recipes that are best suited for you. It is better to avoid doing exercises, but if you are dedicated to doing it at all, then you are required to be kind to your body and choose the ones that require less energy as your body is already trying to adapt to the new form of eating. You know how much you can push yourself and what are the limitations of doing that against your body. Try listening to your body and be kind to it.

Importance of Exercise

In this part, we will be explaining the benefits of exercising.

Feel Happier Now and Always

You want to be happy, right? Well, everyone wants to. You can start that by dedicating some time to exercise. It can do a lot to your body as well as to the mind. From decreasing the feeling of anxiety, stress, and depression to improving your mood, it can do it all. The part of the brain that is responsible for regulating the anxiety and stress undergoes certain changes while you do exercises. It can also make your brain become more sensitive to the hormones norepinephrine and serotonin, which is responsible for relieving the mind from feeling depressed. Endorphin production also increases while you exercise, thus helping you to reduce pain perception and making you feel more positive. Instilling with the thoughts of exercising can even make changes. It is powerful and can even make differences over short periods.

Helps You Lose Weight

Weight gain mainly occurs when a person is inactive. For that reason, it is very important to understand the link between losing weight and exercising to understand its effect on the reduction in weight.

The three main ways in which the body loses energy are exercising, digesting, and maintaining the body for performing functions like breathing and heartbeat. The metabolic rate gets reduced while dieting as the consumption of calories is reduced, which can delay the process of losing weight. The metabolic rate can be increased by exercising, which can burn the desired calories or even more and can even help weight loss.

Additionally, researchers have found that to keep your weight off; you should be combining resistance training with aerobic exercises that can help you lose maximum fat while still maintaining your muscle mass.

Increase in Energy Levels

Healthy people and those who are suffering from medical conditions can boost their energy by exercising regularly.

A study was conducted with thirty-six people who were healthy and were suffering from persistent fatigue. They were asked to exercise regularly for six weeks. And the result was unbelievable. After the time period, they were not complaining about feeling fatigued. It is also helpful for those with the pain of chronic fatigue syndrome. Doing exercise can also boost energy levels. Such patients can easily combine exercise like passive therapies that include stretching and relaxation with their treatments.

This is even found to be true for cancer patients and those suffering AIDS and several scleroses.

For Healthy Bones and Muscles

Maintaining strong bones and muscles is found to be an important role that is played when a person does exercises. Lifting heavy weights can stimulate the building of muscles, coupled with the intake of adequate amounts of protein. This is because hormones are released while doing exercise that promotes the absorption of amino acids by the muscle, which helps them to grow and lessens the breakdown.

With increasing age, people tend to lose their ability to function due to the loss of muscles. This loss can be essentially reduced, and strength can be maintained by practicing regular activities of the body. Gymnastics and playing games like basketball and soccer can promote increased bone density.

Reduce the Risk of Chronic Diseases

Chronic diseases are mainly caused due to the lack of physical activities. But people who have been exercising regularly have shown to improve the insulin sensitivity, composition of the body, and cardiovascular fitness. They have also shown a reduction in the levels of blood fat and blood pressure.

In contrast, people who were not doing fitness workouts regularly were facing significant problems like an increase in belly fat, which increased the risks of heart diseases and were responsible for early deaths.

Enhance Your Memory

The functioning of the brain can be effectively increased by doing regular exercise. This can also improve your thinking skills and protect your memory.

To start with, the rate of the heartbeat is essentially increased while exercising which increases blood flow in the brain cells. Certain hormones are stimulated that improves the growth of brain cells. It also helps to reduce certain diseases that can affect the functioning of the brain.

Exercise is important for aged people who are suffering from inflammation and oxidative stress. Exercise can help to prevent the change in the structure and function of the brain caused by these problems.

Improved Skin Health

The amount of oxidative stress that is produced in your body can affect your skin health. Free radicals cause damage to the cells, which is effectively repaired by the antioxidant defenses of the body. Oxidative stress occurs when these defenses are not able to repair the damages completely. The natural antioxidants that are present can easily be increased by doing moderate exercises, which can protect the cells. The skin cells can also be induced to adopt that can delay the skin aging process by stimulating the flow of blood by doing exercises.

Gain Efficiency in Sleeping Habits

While a person sleeps, all the restorative processes are stimulated by the depletion of the energy that occurs during exercising. The sleeping quality is increased by the increase in the temperature of the body while exercising. Doing moderate to strenuous physical activities regularly has shown to increase the quality of sleep and make them sleep longer who suffer from insomnia. Aged people are also benefited by doing mild exercises suffering from sleeping disorders.

Doing the right kind of exercise and choosing them according to your flexibility will be doing the perfect work in keeping your body fit and helping you get rid of the complications.

Get Rid of Pain

It is debilitating to feel pain, but you may use exercise to reduce them. Chronic pain can be easily reduced by exercising, which can also improve life quality. It can control the pain in many ways, including lowering the pain in the back, treating fibromyalgia, and other disorders in the shoulder.

Doing exercise can also increase your tolerance to pain and decrease the perception of pain.

The Physical Activity Effect

The Sirtfood Diet is about consuming certain products that are designed to promote sustainable weight loss and wellbeing by definition. But with the advantages that you see by practicing the plan, you can fall into the trap of feeling there's no need to exercise. This will be endorsed by many diet books, saying how ineffective exercise is compared with following the right diet for weight loss. And it's real; we can't outdo a bad diet. It's not the approach we saw earlier that was supposed to support weight loss. It's inefficient, and the harmfulness of being too many borders. So, it's that till we see stars or achieve an Olympian's feats, there's no need to pound the treadmill — but what about general everyday movement?

The truth is we are now much less involved than we used to be. The age of technology has ensured physical activity is practically factored out of our daily lives, for all the advancements it has provided. We don't have to mess with the whole process of being involved unless we want to. Forget about weight loss for a second and just glance at the litany of positive health benefits correlated with it. These include reduced risk of cardiovascular disease, stroke, hypertension, type 2 diabetes, osteoporosis, obesity and cancer, and improved mood, sleep, confidence, and a sense of wellbeing.

While many of the benefits of being active are driven by switching on our sirtuin genes, eating Sirtfoods shouldn't be used as a reason to not engage in exercise. Instead, we should understand how active the ideal complement to our Sirtfood intake is. It activates optimum stimulation of the sirtuin, and all the advantages that it provides, just as expected by definition.

What we are talking about here is meeting 150-minute (2 hours and 30 minutes) government guidelines of moderate physical activity a week. A moderate job is the equivalent of a brisk walk. But that doesn't have to be limited to this. Any sport or physical activity you love is fitting. Pleasure and exercise do not have to be mutually exclusive! So, their social aspect enriches squad or group sports even more. It's also about everyday things like taking the bike instead of the car, or getting off the bus one stop earlier, or just parking farther away to increase the distance you've got to walk around. Take the stairs and not the lift. Go outdoors and do gardening. Play in the park with your kids or get more out with the dog. Everything counts. Everything that has you up and moving will activate your sirtuin genes regularly and at moderate intensity, enhancing the benefits of the Sirtfood Diet.

Engaging in physical activity and eating a diet high in Sirtfood brings the buck the full sirtuin click. All it takes to achieve the benefit of physical activity is the equivalent of a quick 30-minute stroll five days a week.

Chapter 9: Pros and Cons of sirtfood diet

PROS

It Improves Powerful Exercise

Normal exercise is perhaps the best thing you can accomplish for your health and doing some direct exercise will improve the weight loss and medical advantages of Phase 1 of the diet. When in doubt, we urge you to proceed with your typical degree of activity and physical action through the initial seven days of the Sirtfood Diet. Be that as it may, we recommend remaining inside your typical safe place, since delayed or excessively extreme exercise may just place a lot of weight on the body for this period. Tune in to your body. There's no compelling reason to drive yourself to accomplish more exercise during Phase 1; let the Sirtfoods accomplish the difficult work.

It can be applied for underweight

A decent method to see whether you are underweight is to figure your weight file or BMI. For whatever length of time that you know your height and weight, you can without much of a stretch decide this by utilizing one of the various BMI adding machines on the web. In the event that your BMI is 18.5 or less, we don't suggest that you leave on Phase 1 of the eating routine. On the off chance that your BMI is somewhere in the range of 18.5 and 20, we would at present urge alert, since following the diet may imply that your BMI falls beneath 18.5. While numerous individuals seek to be super-thin, actually being underweight can adversely influence numerous parts of health, adding to a brought down safe structure, a raised danger of osteoporosis (debilitating of the bones), and ripeness issues. While we don't suggest Phase 1 of the diet on the off chance that you are underweight, we do at present energize the combination of a lot of Sirtfoods into a decent method of eating with the goal that all the medical advantages of these foods can be harvested.

Be that as it may, in the event that you are thin however have a BMI in the sound range (20–25), there is literally nothing preventing you from beginning. A larger part of the members engaged with the pilot preliminary had BMIs in the sound range, yet still lost great measures of weight and turned out to be progressively conditioned. Critically, a considerable lot of them announced a noteworthy improvement in energy levels, essentialness, and appearance. Recall that the Sirtfood Diet is tied in with advancing health as much for what it's worth about getting in shape.

Please, do not start the Sirtfood or any diet without a medical advice and without a physician following you in your journey.

Appropriate For weight loss

Being obese expands the danger of various constant medical issues, yet these are the very ailments that Sirtfoods help to secure against.

Provides Fiber

Numerous Sirtfoods are normally rich in fiber. Onions, garlic, and pecans are striking sources, with buckwheat and Medjool dates truly sticking out, implying that a Sirtfood-rich diet doesn't miss the mark in the fiber division. In any event, during Phase 1, when food utilization is decreased, the vast majority of us will in any case be eating a fiber amount we are utilized to, particularly on the off chance that we pick the plans that contain buckwheat, beans, and lentils from the menu choices. In any case, for others known to be powerless to stomach issues like obstruction without higher fiber admissions, during Phase 1, particularly Days 1 to 3, an appropriate fiber supplement can be thought of, which ought to be examined with your social insurance proficient.

CONS

Ineffective with Medication

The Sirtfood Diet is reasonable for the vast majority, but since of its amazing impacts on fat burning and health, it can change certain sickness forms and the activities of drug recommended by your doctor.

Discuss about this diet with your doctor first before trying it. The odds are it will be fine and really of significant advantage for you, yet it's critical to check.

Can't be administered during pregnancy or breastfeeding

Try not to follow the Sirtfood Diet on the off chance that you are attempting to imagine or in the event that you are pregnant or breastfeeding. It is a ground-breaking weight loss diet, which makes it inadmissible. Notwithstanding, don't be put off eating a lot of Sirtfoods, since these are astoundingly solid foods to incorporate as a major aspect of a reasonable and fluctuated diet for pregnancy. You will need to dodge red wine, because of its liquor substance, and cutoff energized things, for example, espresso, green tea, and cocoa so as not to surpass 200 milligrams for each day of caffeine during pregnancy (one cup of moment espresso normally contains around 100 milligrams of caffeine). Proposals are not to surpass four cups of green tea day by day and to maintain a strategic distance from matcha out and out. Other than that, you're allowed to receive the benefits of incorporating Sirtfoods in your diet.

Diet may cause mild symptoms

Phase 1 of the Sirtfood Diet gives amazing normally happening food mixes in quantities that the vast majority would not get in their ordinary eating routine, and certain individuals can respond as they adjust to this sensational wholesome change. This can incorporate indications, for example, a mild headache or tiredness, in spite of the fact that as far as we can tell these impacts are minor and fleeting.

Obviously, if side effects are extreme or give you purpose behind concern, we suggest you look for clinical counsel. No different manifestations have never been seen other than incidental gentle side effects that resolve rapidly, and inside a couple of days a great many people discover they have a restored feeling of energy, power, and healthiness.

The Sirtfood diet is superfluously prohibitive, eating 1/200 calories daily is excessively prohibitive for some individuals

The diet likewise requires drinking up to three green juices for each day. In spite of the fact that juices can be a decent wellspring of nutrients and minerals, they are likewise a wellspring of sugar and contain practically none of the solid fiber found in entire leafy foods

Tasting juice for the duration of the day is a poorly conceived notion for your glucose and teeth

The way that the diet is exceptionally restricted in calories and food decisions, it is more than likely inadequate in protein, nutrients and minerals, particularly during the main stage.

High beginning expenses of buying a juicer, the book and some uncommon and costly fixings, just as the tedious expenses of setting up specific meals and juices

Diet gets unworkable and unreasonable for some individuals or on the other hand a diabetic individual, calorie limitation and utilization of juice during the primary days of the diet can prompt perilous changes in glucose levels

During the main stage, you may encounter opposite reactions, for example, weariness, tipsiness and touchiness because of the calorie limitation

Chapter 10: What Next? The Sirtfood Diet in the Long Term

After the Two Phases

Congratulations, all stages of the Sirtfood Diet have now finished! Just let's take stock of what you have achieved. You've entered the hyper-success process, achieving weight loss in the area of 7 pounds, which probably includes an attractive increase in muscle. You also maintained your weight loss throughout the fourteen-day maintenance phase and further strengthened the body composition. Perhaps notably, you have marked the beginning of your transformation of wellness. You took a stand against the tide of ill health, which strikes as often as we get older. The life you have decided for yourself is enhanced strength, productivity, and health.

By now, you'll be familiar with the top twenty Sirtfoods, and you've gained a sense of how powerful they are. Not only that, but you'll also probably have become quite good at including them in your diet and loving them. For the sustained weight loss and health, they offer, these items must stay a prominent feature in your everyday eating regimen. But still, they're just twenty foods, and after all, the spice of life is variety. What next, then? We'll give you the blueprint for lifelong health in the next pages.

It's about getting your body in perfect balance with a diet that's suitable and sustainable for everyone and providing all the nutrients we need that enhance our health. It's about keeping on reaping the Sirtfood Diet's weight-loss rewards using the very best foods nature has to offer.

We've seen why Sirtfoods are so beneficial: certain plants have sophisticated stress-response mechanisms that generate compounds that trigger sirtuins— the same fasting and exercise-activated fat-burning and durability mechanism in the body. The greater the quantity of these compounds produced by plants in response to stress, the higher the value we derive from their feeding. Our list of the top twenty Sirtfoods is made up of the foods that stand out because they are particularly packed full of these compounds, and hence the foods that have the most exceptional ability to impact body composition and wellbeing. But foods ' sirtuin-activating results aren't a concept of all or nothing. There are a lot of other plants that produce moderate levels of sirtuin-activating nutrients, and by eating these liberally, we encourage you to expand the variety and diversity of your diet. The Sirtfood Diet is all about inclusion, and the greater the range of sirtuin-activating items that can be integrated into the diet. Especially if that means you will obtain from your meals even more of your favorite foods to increase pleasure and enjoyment.

Let's use the workout comparison. The top twenty Sirtfoods are the (much more pleasurable) equivalent of sweating it out at the gym, with Phase 1 being the "boot camp." By contrast, eating those other foods with more moderate levels of sirtuin-activating nutrients is like reaping the rewards of going out for a good walk. Contrast that to the typical diet that has a nutritional value equal to sitting all day on the couch watching Television. Yeah, sweating it out in the gym is fine, but if that is all you do, you will quickly get fed up with it. The walk should also be welcomed, especially if it means that you don't just choose to sit on the sofa.

For e.g., in our top twenty Sirtfoods, if we look more broadly at berries as a food group, we find that they have metabolic health benefits as well as healthy aging. Reviewing their nutritional content, we note that other berries such as blackberries, black currants, blueberries, and raspberries also have significant amounts of nutrients that cause sirtuins.

The same holds with nuts. Notwithstanding their calorific material, nuts are so effective that they promote weight loss and help shift inches from the waist. This is in addition to cutting chronic disease risk. Though walnuts are our champion nut, nutrients that trigger sirtuin can also be found in chestnuts, pecans, pistachios, and even peanuts.

Instead, we turn our attention to food. Throughout recent years there has been in several areas an increasing aversion to grains. Studies, however, link whole grain consumption with decreased inflammation, diabetes, heart disease, and cancer. Although they do not equal the pseudo-grain buckwheat Sirtfood qualifications, we do see the existence of substantial sirtuin-activating nutrients in other whole grains. And needless to say, their sirtuin-activating nutrient quality is decimated when whole grains are converted into refined "clean" forms. Such modified models are quite dangerous groups and are interested in a number of state-of-the-art health problems. We're not saying you can never eat them, but instead, you're going to be much better off sticking to the whole-grain version whenever possible.

With the likes of goji berries and chia seeds possessing Sirtfood powers, also notorious "superfoods" get on the bandwagon. That is most likely the unwitting reason for the health benefits they have observed. While it does imply that they are healthy for us to consume, we do know that there are more accessible, more available, and better options out there, so don't feel compelled to get on that specific bandwagon! We see the same trend across a lot of food categories. Unsurprisingly, the foods that research has developed are usually good for us, and we should be consuming more of them. Below we mentioned about forty foods that we discovered have Sirtfood properties too. We actively encourage you to include these foods to maintain and continue your weight loss and wellbeing as you expand your diet repertoire.

- Vegetables
- Artichokes
- Asparagus
- Broccoli
- Frisée
- Green beans
- Shallots
- Watercress
- White onions
- Yellow endive
- Fruits
- Apples
- Blackberries
- Black currants

- Black plums
- Cranberries
- Grains and pseudo-grains
- Popcorn
- Quinoa
- Whole-wheat flour
- Beans
- Fava beans
- White beans (e.g., cannellini or navy)
- Beverages
- Black tea
- White tea

Power of Protein

A high protein diet is one of the most popular diets of the last few years. Higher protein intake while dieting has been shown to encourage satiety, sustain metabolism, and reduce muscle mass loss. But it's when they pair Sirtfoods with protein that things get brought to a whole new level. Protein is, as you may remember, a necessary addition in a diet based on Sirtfood to gain maximum benefits. Protein consists of amino acids, and it is a particular amino acid, leucine, which effectively complements Sirt-foods ' behavior, strengthening their effects. This is done primarily by changing our cellular environment so that our diet's sirtuin-activating nutrients work much more effectively. It ensures we get the best result from a Sirtfood-rich meal, which is paired with protein-based in leucine. Leucine's main dietary sources contain red meat, pork, fruit, vegetables, milk, and dairy products.

The Power of Three

The omega-3 long-chain fatty acids EPA and DHA are the second major category of nutrients that effectively complement Sirtfoods. Omega-3s have been the coveted natural wellbeing global favorite for years. What we didn't know before, which we are doing now, is that they also improve the activation of a group of sirtuin genes in the body that is directly linked to longevity. It makes them the perfect match for Sirtfoods.

Omega-3s have potent effects in decreasing inflammation and lowering fat blood levels. To that, we can add additional heart-healthy effects: rendering the blood less likely to pool, stabilizing the heart's electrical activity, and lowering blood pressure. Even the pharmaceutical industry now looks to them as an aid in the war against cardiac disease. And that is not where the litany of benefits ends. Omega-3s also have an effect on the way we perceive, having been shown to boost the outlook and help stave off dementia.

When we speak about omega-3s, we're thinking primarily about eating fish, particularly oily types, because no other dietary source comes close to supplying the significant levels of EPA and DHA that we need. And to see the benefits, all we need is two servings of fish a week, with an emphasis on oily fish. Sadly, the United States is not a country of big fish eaters, and that is accomplished by less than one in five Americans. As a result, our intake of the precious EPA and DHA is appallingly short.

Plant foods, including almonds, beans, and green leafy vegetables, often produce omega-3 but in a form called alpha-linolenic acid, which must be processed into EPA or DHA in the body. This conversion process is poor, meaning that alpha-linolenic acid delivers a negligible amount of our needs for omega-3. Even with the wonderful advantages of Sirtfoods, we shouldn't forget the added value that drinking adequate omega-3 fats provides. In that order, the best sources of omega-3 fish are herring, sardines, salmon, trout, and mackerel. While fresh tuna is naturally high, too, the tinned version loses the majority of the omega-3. And a replacement of DHA-enriched microalgae (up to 300 milligrams a day) is also recommended for vegetarians and vegans, though food foods should still be integrated into the diet.

Can A SirtFood Provide it All?

Our focus so far has been solely on Sirtfoods and reaping their maximum benefits in order to achieve the body we want and powerfully boost our health in the process. But is this a reasonable, long-term dietary solution to be taken? After all, there is more to diet than pure nutrients that trigger sirtuin. What about all the vitamins, minerals, and fibers that are also important to our wellbeing, and the diets that we should consume to satisfy such demands?

Based on sirtfood diets, augmented by protein-rich foods and omega-3 outlets, fulfill dietary needs across the entire spectrum of essential nutrients— much more so than any other diet does. They use kale, for example, because it is a good sirtfood, but it is a great source of vitamins C, folate, and manganese, calcium, Vitamin K, and magnesium minerals. Kale is also a tremendous source of carotenoids lutein and zeaxanthin, both of which are critical for eye health, as well as immune-boosting beta-carotene.

Walnuts are also rich in minerals such as magnesium, copper, zinc, manganese, calcium, and iron, as well as fiber. Buckwheat is made of manganese, magnesium, zinc, potassium, and cotton. Tick the boxes of the onions for vitamin B6, folate, potassium, and food. Yet bananas, as well as potassium yet manganese, are good sources of vitamin C. And so, it begins. When you broaden your menu to include the expanded Sirtfood list and leave space for all the other good foods you enjoy eating, unwittingly, what you're going to end up with is a diet that's far richer in vitamins, nutrients, and fiber than you've ever had before. What Sirtfoods offers is a missing food group that changes the landscape of how we judge how good foods are for us, and how we eat a genuinely full diet.

Chapter 11: Question and Answers

Do questions and answer to possible doubts or worries of the reader

1. Should I exercise while on the Sirtfood diet?

Yes, of course! Light workouts increase the efficiency of the sirtfood diet and help you progress faster on your journey to losing weight, achieving enhanced mental clarity, and reducing the risk of long-term chronic diseases. So, keep your workouts simple, limit physical exertion, but try as much as possible to exercise every single day.

2. Can the Sirtfood Diet rectify extreme obesity?

A lot of people believe that diets only work for overweight people, and full-blown obesity can only be corrected by surgical procedures. The decision of whether you need surgery to remove the excess fat deposits would depend on your doctor. However, if your cardiac health is not in immediate danger, the sirtfood diet can help you to make immense progress in the long run by helping you to consistently shed your fat deposits while consolidating on your muscle mass gains.

3. Should I continue with the Sirtfood Diet after hitting my Target Weight?

The aim of the sirtfood diet is to help you to build a healthy routine that would allow you to stay healthy and disease-free in the long term. Even after reaching your target weight, try as much as possible to keep sirtfoods dominant in your diet, and avoid forbidden foods such as alcohol and processed sugar as much as possible. Sticking to the basic rules will help prevent you from gaining excess weight again. Remember to also keep exercising and going for regular medical check-ups if necessary.

4. How many times should I drink the Sirtfood Green Juice per day?

This is quite a common question among people who are just getting familiar with the sirtfood diet. Because of the intense calorie restriction in the first three days of phase one, it is recommended that you consume three cups of the sirtfood green juice per day for those three days. For the subsequent four days of Phase One, the sirtfood juice can be consumed twice per day. From phase 2 onwards, it is okay to keep the consumption of the juice at one cup per day; to be taken before breakfast in the morning to help give you your daily dose of green vitality.

5. Can I embark on the Sirtfood Diet if I'm on special medication?

If you are using meds, then you might need to talk to your doctor before starting the diet. However, even if your meds wouldn't allow you to go through the intense calorie restrictions of phase one, you can still incorporate sirtfoods into your diet and enjoy the amazing goodness that comes from consuming these foods.

6. Can Pregnant women embark on the sirtfood diet?

Once again, try as much as possible to talk to your physician before making any decisions on the sirtfood diet as a pregnant woman. Your baby requires enough nutrition as possible and restricting calories in this delicate stage may not be such a good idea. You can, however, incorporate the sirtfoods into your diet also. Children also should not embark on a full-scale diet. Instead, they should just be fed a lot of sirtfoods.

7. Must I complete the Seven-day period of Phase One?

For superlative execution, it is recommended that the seven-day period for phase One be completed. However, if for health reasons or any other cogent excuse, you cannot complete the full days, then try to stick to the rules of phase One for a minimum of five days to reap the rewards of the sirtfood diet. If you have a special medical condition such as ulcers, talk to your doctor before embarking on this diet, or simply just incorporate sirtfoods into your regular diet. Note that if you want to repeat the first phase of the diet, you have to wait for a month before going through that seven-day regimen again.

8. Can Children Eat Sirtfoods?

There are powerful sirtfoods, most of which are safe for children. Obviously, children should avoid wine, coffee, and other highly caffeinated foods, such as matcha. On the other hand, children can enjoy sirtuin-rich foods such as cabbage, eggplant, blueberries, and dates with their regular balanced diet.

Yet, while children can enjoy most sirtuin-rich foods, that is not the same as to say that they can practice the Sirt diet. This diet plan is not designed for children, and it does not fit the needs of their growing bodies. Practicing this diet plan could not only negatively affect them physically, but it could damage their mental health for years to come. Anyone can develop an eating disorder, but it is especially true for children. If you want your child to eat well, ensure they eat a wide range of foods, as recommended by their doctor, and you can simply include an abundance of sirtuin-rich foods into what they are already eating. Leave the focus on eating healthfully and not losing weight. Even if your child's doctor does want them to lose weight, you don't need to make the child aware of this fact. You can help guide them along with a healthy lifestyle, teaching them how to eat well and stay active through sports and play, and the weight will come off naturally without placing an unneeded burden on their small shoulders.

For similar reasons, you can include sirtfoods in a balanced diet while pregnant, but you should avoid practicing the Sirt diet when you are pregnant. It doesn't contain the nutrition requirements for either a pregnant woman or a growing baby. Save the diet for after you have delivered a healthy baby, and both you and your child will be healthy and happy.

9. Can I Exercise During Phase One?

If you use exercise during either phase one or two, you can increase weight loss and health benefits. While you shouldn't work at pushing the limits during phase one, you can continue your normal workout routine and physical activity. It is important to stay within your active comfort zone during this time, as physical exertion more than you are accustomed to will be especially difficult while you are restricting your calories. It will not only wear you out, but it can also make you dizzy, more prone to injury, and physically and mentally exhausted. This is a common symptom whenever a person pushes their limits while restricting calories, but it is something you should avoid.

If you are used to doing yoga and a spin class a few times a week, keep it up! If you are used to running a few miles a day, have at it! Do what you and your body are comfortable with, and as your doctor advises, and you should be fine.

10. I'm Already Thin. Can I Still Follow The Diet?

Whether or not you can follow the first phase of the Sirt diet will depend just how thin you already are. While a person who is overweight or well within a healthy weight can practice the first phase, nobody who is clinically underweight should. You can know whether or not you are underweight by calculating your Body Mass Index, or BMI. You can find many BMI calculators online, and if yours is at nineteen points or below, you should avoid the first phase. It is always a good idea to ask your doctor both if it is safe for you to lose weight, and if the Sirt diet is safe for your individual condition. While the Sirt diet may generally be safe, for people with certain illnesses, it may not be the case.

While it is understandable to desire to be even thinner, even if you already are thin, pushing yourself past the point of being underweight is incredibly unhealthy, both physically and mentally. This fits into the category of disordered eating and can cause you a lot of harm.

Some of the side effects of pushing your body to extreme weight loss include bone loss and osteoporosis, lowered immune system, fertility problems, and an increased risk of disease. If you want to benefit from the health of the Sirt diet and are underweight, instead consume, however many calories, your doctor recommends, along with plenty of sirtfoods. This will ensure you maintain a healthy weight while also receiving the benefits that sirtuins have to offer.

If you are thin, but still at a BMI of twenty to twenty-five, then you should be safe beginning the Sirt diet, unless otherwise instructed by your doctor.

11. Can You Eat Meat and Dairy on The Sirtfood Diet?

In many recipes, we choose to use sirtfood sources of protein, such as soy, walnuts, and buckwheat. However, this does not mean that you aren't allowed to enjoy meat on the Sirt diet. Sure, it's easy to enjoy a vegan or vegetarian Sirt diet, but if you love your sources of meat, then you don't have to give them up. Protein is an essential aspect of the Sirt diet to preserve muscle tone, and whether you consume only plant-based proteins, or a mixture of plant and animal-based proteins is completely up to you. And, just as you can enjoy meat, you can also enjoy moderate consumption of dairy.

Some meats can actually help you better utilize the sirtfoods you eat. This is because the amino acid leucine is able to enhance the effect of sirtfoods. You can find this amino acid in chicken, beef, pork, fish, eggs, dairy, and tofu.

12. Can I Drink Red Wine during Phase One?

As your calories will be so limited during the first phase, it is not recommended to drink alcohol during this phase. However, you can enjoy it in moderation during phase two and the maintenance phase.

Then sirtfood diet isn't science-based

Even though there's some contentious research in regard to the advantages of sirtuins, there is little to no research in regard to a particular sirtfood dietary plan. In any case, we have many tips in place which were thoroughly researched and analyzed for many years. If you should be lost about which "healthy food" is, then this can be really a greater place to get started out.

It is totally fine if you'd like to add some sirtfoods in an eating program. After all, foods such as green tea extract, tea, dark chocolate, and kale all are important to a nutritious eating pattern! But staying with a schedule with such strict pass-or-fail conditions is unrealistic and maybe bad for your relationship with food. By incorporating a diet plan that is satisfying and focused on eating mindfully, you are going to be in a position to set a long-term and sustainable love with food. Cheers to this!

Conclusion

The Sirtfood Diet is all about consuming the right foods and getting fast consequences. It is the maximum popular eating regimen to date, ably overturning outcomes that made the Dukan and Paleo famous. This food plan entails meals with large quantities of Sirtuin activators.

These activators switch on the body's skinny gene pathways by way of approach of exercising and fasting for you to burn fats, enhance muscles, and beautify fitness. The diet regime includes meals and advice that might maintain you off from the burden you lost all through the first week of this system and integrating extra Sirtfoods to your meals as you go along.

With around 650 million overweight adults around the world, it's crucial to find healthful meals and doable exercising programs, don't throw away the whole thing you love and don't must exercise all the time. Time. Week. The Sirtfood weight loss program does just that: The idea is that certain meals set off the "lean gene" pathways that are generally activated by way of fasting and workout.

As soon as the weight loss program becomes a way of life during exercising, it is critical to eat protein one hour after a workout preferably. The protein repairs muscles after exercising, relieve ache, and can sell regeneration. There are loads of recipes that include proteins best for post-exercise consumption, e.g., For example, B. Sirt Chili con Carne or turmeric-chicken-kale salad. If you want something lighter, you can attempt the Sirt Blueberry smoothie and upload protein powder for extra benefits. The type of health you exercise is up to you. However, in case you are educated at home, you could pick while you want to exercise, what sorts of sporting events are right for you, and are quick and convenient.

Take note that you should maintain the weight loss results through Phase 2 and continue to lose weight gradually. Also, the one striking thing we've seen with the Sirtfood Diet is that most or all of the weight people lose is from fat and that many put some muscle on. So, we would like to warn you again not to measure your success solely based on the numbers. Look in the mirror to see if you look leaner and more toned, see how well your clothes fit and lap up the compliments you'll get from others.

The Sirtfood diet is a first-rate way to trade your consuming habits, lose weight, and experience healthier. The first few weeks may be difficult. However, it's critical to test which meals are high-quality to devour and which delicious recipes are proper for you. Be type to yourself for the first few weeks, as your body adapts and trains while you need to. If you are already exercising moderately or intensively, you'll be able to preserve as standard or manipulate your health primarily based on the exchange in diet. As with any change in food plan and workout, it all depends on the individual and what kind of effort you can make.

For other 302 recipes you can buy my book "SIRTFOOD DIET COOKBOOK".

Made in the USA
Monee, IL
04 February 2022